JUST
Another
MINUTE

JUST *Another* MINUTE

MORE GLIMPSES OF OUR GREAT CANADIAN HERITAGE

Marsha Boulton

Little, Brown and Company (Canada) Limited
Boston • New York • Toronto • London

Canadian Cataloguing In Publication Data

Boulton, Marsha
    Just another minute: more glimpses of our great Canadian heritage

ISBN 0-316-10418-3

1. Canada – History – Miscellanea.   2. Questions and answers. I. Title.

FC176.B67 1997   971   C97 – 930158–0
F1026.B67 1997

Cover design by 4 Eyes

Interior design and page composition
by Andrew Smith Graphics Inc.

Printed and bound in Canada by Best Book Manufacturers

Little, Brown and Company (Canada) Limited
148 Yorkville Avenue
Toronto, ON, M5R 1C2

10   9   8   7   6   5   4   3   2   1

TABLE OF CONTENTS

ACKNOWLEDGEMENTS 9

1. ORIGINS   15

1497: HATS OFF TO THE BEAVER 16
Castor canadensis — our national rodent

1535: THE *ANNEDA* SOLUTION 20
Solving the scurrilous scourge of scurvy

1606: EASIER SAID THAN DONE 24
Marc Lescarbot searches for a haven in the wilderness

1663: THE FATTEST AND THE REST 27
Women are the clue to population

1851: *EÒIN A' CHUAN* 31
Norman MacLeod leads Gaelic "Sea Birds" on a mass migration

1877: BY MANY NAMES SHALL YOU KNOW HIM 36
Crowfoot — the relinquishing of a birthright

1914: WHO IS WHAT AND WHAT IS WHO 41
How a Canadian bear became Winnie the Pooh

1923: AN ALLELUIA IN THE SKY 45
The crackling candle dragon of the Northern dawn

2. HEROES, HEROINES AND THE ODD VILLAIN   49

1692: HOLDING THE FORT 50
The glorious inclination of Madeleine de Verchères

1856: THE HANGING JUDGE 53
Matthew Begbie — have gavel will travel

1867: CAPTAIN COURAGEOUS 56
William Jackman follows the family creed to heroism

1874: NO NUDDER LIKE HIM 59
Jerry Potts of the North-West Mounted Police

1878: WHERE'S JOE'S BEEF? 62
Charles McKiernan — the generous innkeeper

1910: LEAVE IT TO THE BEAVER 65
Max Aitken makes hay whether or not the sun shines

1938: THE SITDOWNERS 71
Steve Brodie leads a transients' strike

1946: TICKLING THE DRAGON'S TAIL 77
Louis Slotin's supercritical sacrifice

1955: *EKOKTOEGEE* 80
Judge Sissons listens to the Inuit

3. HERSTORY   87

1794: A ROYAL CANADIAN LOVE STORY 88
Madame St. Laurent and her Prince in Halifax

1857: NO SEX PLEASE, WE'RE DOCTORS 93
The posthumous unmasking of Dr. Barry

1858: A SPY FOR THE YANKEES 97
Sarah Emma Edmonds crosses more than enemy lines

1882: THE RIGHT TO BE BEAUTIFUL 101
Elizabeth Arden changes the face of women

1897: FOR HOME AND COUNTRY 106
Adelaide Hoodless — Woman of Vision

1898: OUR LADY OF THE SOURDOUGH 109
Martha Black's "beloved Yukon" adventure

1915: "FOR THERE SHALL BE A PERFORMANCE" 112
Sister Aimee Semple McPherson finds her voice.

4. SPORTS   117

1892: TURN-OF-THE-CENTURY TERMINATOR .. 118
Louis Cyr and eighteen fat men

1904: SINGING ON THE GREENS 122
George S. Lyon — Canada's swingingest Olympian

1907: THE RUNNING MAN 125
Tom "Wildfire" Longboat gives his everything

1909: JUST FOR THE FUN OF IT 129
Tommy Ryan turns ten-pins into five

1912: TURN HIM LOOSE! 133
Tom Three Persons tames Cyclone

1922: THE BIG TRAIN THAT COULD 136
All-round all-star Lionel Conacher

1928: GILDING THE SASKATOON LILY 139
Ethel Catherwood flies through the air

5. ADVENTURE, DISCOVERY AND ART   143

1578: FOOLS RUSH IN 144
Martin Frobisher leads the first gold rush

1842: A HATFUL OF GRAIN 148
David Fife reaps what he sows

1896: THE GREAT CANADIAN KISSER 151
May Irwin delivers a fifty-foot pucker

1913: ONE WITH THE SOIL 154
Charles Noble's blade takes root on the prairies

1914: THE PIE MAN 159
Mack Sennett — the king of comedy

1915: BORN OF FIRE AND BLOOD 163
John McCrae's poem of sacrifice and challenge

1929: SHE DID IT HER WAY 166
La Bolduc — First Lady of *Chanson*

1930: THE WONDER MUSH REVOLUTION 169
Pablum — the glop that makes you grow

**6. TRANSPORTATION AND
COMMUNICATION**   173

1862: HUMPS ALONG THE FRASER 174
Camels stink in the Cariboo gold rush

1876: THAT LONG DISTANCE FEELING 178
Phoning and flying with Mr. and Mrs. Bell

1898: PRESS PASS 110 182
Kit Coleman — war correspondent

1900: RADIO MAN 187
Reginald Fessenden — the father of radio

1915: THE MAVERICK MUSE OF THE WEST . . . 191
Uncorking the conscience of Bob "Eye-Opener"
Edwards

1921: "JUST ONCE MORE" 194
The unforgettable *Bluenose*

1929: THE PICASSO OF BUSH PILOTS 198
"Punch" Dickins wings it with style

ACKNOWLEDGEMENTS

It has been said that history is a fragile thing. There are many reasons to ignore the past. The modern world is far too much with us. Canadian history is boring, or it's inaccessible or "why bother, what's in it for me?" is sometimes an impossible question to answer.

One of my personal heroes, suffragette author, politician and "hyena in petticoats" Nellie McClung, observed that, "People must know the past, to understand the present and to face the future." If I needed any better reason to compile a book like this, I do not know what it could be. I certainly could not express the sentiment any better.

The anecdotal history you will find in these pages is not scholarly, although an epic legion of archivists, advisors and direct descendants have assisted me immeasurably in matters of fact.

These stories are capsules, which may be easily taken one at a time as glimpses into the character of the builders and the ingredients that comprise the building blocks of our country. Allan Fotheringham mischeivously described my first volume, *Just A Minute!* as a great bathroom book. I took that as an enormous compliment.

To me the most memorable gateway to history is personality, and I constantly strive to articulate its enormous variety. The characters that populate our past run the gamut from rogues to romantics, from poets to poseurs. Be it a hero who braves the icy waves off Newfoundland to save lives, a socialite who heads up the Klondike trail or a farmer who creates a better plough, these brief stories are intended as illuminations of our collective consciousness.

Some of the stories you will recognize in part from the exposure they have garnered on television and in cinemas as "Heritage Minutes." As in *Just A Minute!* what you will find here is an elaboration on the background to some of those stories that cannot be told in sixty seconds. In this regard, I owe a debt of gratitude to the Heritage Project and its creative director — my friend and colleague — Patrick Watson, who have put as much money and effort into advertising Canadian history as the breweries have put into selling beer.

Many individuals have assisted me in gathering information for this book. They include people such as Winnipeg's Fred Colebourn, the son of the soldier who adopted that greatest of all Canadian bears — Winnie the Pooh. In my hometown of Mount Forest, Ontario, I found that one of the local barbers, Jim McLuhan, had a collection of personal reminiscences of the evangelist Aimee Semple McPherson's early crusades that he had gathered from townfolk who remembered her visit.

Organizations from the Women's Institute to the Five-Pin Bowling Association and the Canadian Rodeo Historical Association have supplied me with information and inspiration.

The Kamloops Museum helped me wrestle with the esoterica of Cariboo camels and the Hospital for Sick Children provided a profile on Pablum.

In every corner, nook and cranny of Canada I have found archivists, local historical boards and librarians who were more than willing to indulge my obsession for uncovering stories that need telling. This book is dedicated to their cooperative spirit and integrity. I salute them.

History can be great fun but there are times when I have found the tragedy of it all overwhelming. Anguished by some horror of Canadian wartime experience or traumatized by some tale of unconscionable injustice, I have often turned to nature and the solace of my farm.

My companion, Stephen Williams, is owed a bouquet of gratitude for helping me to maintain that sanctuary and, with it, a sense of humour. Thanks also to my good neighbours, the Houstons, who care for my livestock and land when I suddenly hit the road in hot pursuit of yet another story.

My publisher, Kim McArthur, obviously shares my enthusiasm for Canadian history. But few are aware that not so long ago she achieved a gold medal in the subject during her student days at the University of Western Ontario. When I think that I have uncovered another diamond-in-the-rough, Kim has been a gifted arbiter of what is dross and what is gloss. Little, Brown's Laura Cameron has held my hand with grace through the publicity process, and her colleague, Wilf Clark, has proved to be an able marketer and an amiable friend.

Likewise, my agent, Bruce Westwood, and the team at Westwood Creative Artists have offered unflagging support — even when I have threatened to dominate other people's dinner parties with astounding facts about beavers.

For the past year, it has been my privilege and pleasure to travel throughout Canada as a Canadian Club speaker. Canadian Clubs are exactly what the name would suggest, an organization of citizens with a common interest in knowing more about this country and the issues that make it tick.

In conjunction with that tour, Canada's National Historical Society sponsored the attendance of high-school students at dinners and luncheons when I was speaking. I met hundreds of students and their teachers and discovered in them a real and vital interest in Canadian history. Repeatedly, I have been told that it is difficult for students to access history, to find time for it in their studies, and to determine how it relates to getting a job.

As T.S. Eliot wrote in *Four Quartets*:

> *Time present and time past*
> *Are both perhaps present in time future.*
> *And time future contained in time past.*
> *If all time is eternally present*
> *All time is unredeemable.*

It is this "unredeemability" that makes time and one's sense of it so precious and valuable. History combines elements of language, geography and culture with human endeavour. From fact, it inspires fiction, drama and poetry. Its lessons are much more than dry dates to be memorized. If it is perceived as an epic adventure — a story running in a continual loop — which can be dipped into at any given time, then it becomes immediately accessible, relevant and exciting. When time is truly perceived as "unredeemable" we make time for it.

One well-possessed young man approached me after a speech. He advised me that although he planned to pursue a degree in business administration, he was considering adding a history course to his studies. Of course, I told him that was admirable, but he was surprised when I told him that he might also find it helpful when he entered the business world.

The world of business is every hectare as much a battlefield as the Plains of Abraham, and the only true way to formulate a winning strategy may well be to see it in the context of military battles. In fact, I said, I suppose history could easily be seen as the sum total of all battles lost and won and their consequences. The young man smiled. All of a sudden, history had a reason to be part of his life. It can be as simple as that.

PART ONE

ORIGINS

HATS OFF TO THE BEAVER

THE *ANNEDA* SOLUTION

EASIER SAID THAN DONE

THE FATTEST AND THE REST

EÒIN A' CHUAN

BY MANY NAMES SHALL YOU KNOW HIM

WHO IS WHAT AND WHAT IS WHO

AN ALLELUIA IN THE SKY

HATS OFF TO THE BEAVER

CASTOR CANADENSIS — OUR NATIONAL RODENT

New World, 1497 — If British hatmakers had been watching closely when Giovanni Caboto (John Cabot) made his landmark voyages to the New World in 1497 and 1498, the course of history might have changed. As it was, Cabot's discovery of cod in quantity off the shores of Newfoundland and New Brunswick was initially more interesting than the beaver furs he brought back to England. It took French explorers, and French fashion mavens, to recognize in the beaver a prize that would shape the future of a nation. Once word got out, it was open season on the beaver.

Native tribes used the beaver in their names and emblems long before Europeans decided to make them into hats. The Onondagas had a Beaver clan, while the Amihona, an Algonkian tribe, were known as "People of the Beaver." On the Pacific Coast, the Tsimshian and Haida claimed the beaver as their totem.

In subsequent symbolic use, *Castor canadensis* has been featured on the first Canadian stamp, the Three Penny Beaver. Its image shares the nickel coin with that of the monarch. Patriotic posters of the Second World War show the buck-toothed creature gnawing down a tree in which a terrified Adolf Hitler perches. The ubiquitous beaver is a feature in more than one thousand place names in Canada. Yet at one time the beaver neared extinction, saved in part by the silkworm, whose handiwork replaced beaver felt as the fabric of choice for nineteenth-century hats.

Hatters went quite literally mad over the fur of the beaver. Most prized of all was a pre-conditioned beaver pelt known as *castor gras d'hiver*. These were prime winter beaver pelts, skinned by native women who scraped the inner sides, rubbed them with animal marrow and cut them into manageable rectangles that were sewn together with moose sinews. Native peoples wore beaver robes with the fur against their flesh. Over a period of months, the long "guard" hairs in the fur, already loosened by the initial scraping, would fall away leaving only the downy underfur.

Felt was made by removing this duvet coat from the pelt and rolling or pounding it flat. Then it was bonded with shellac for shaping into a variety of trendy headgear from the Stetson-like *copatain* hat of the 1500s to the 1700s *tricorne*. The virtue of beaver over other furs lay in the microscopic barbs in the hairs that hooked together so a minimum of bond was required to create a fine "bever hatte."

News that their old clothes could be bartered for a bounty of foreign goods from kettles to knives came as some surprise to the natives. "You glory ... in our miserable suits of beaver which can no longer be of use to us," one Micmac is reported to have remarked. What he did not know was that the traders were making a profit of up to 2,000 percent.

The beaver was a national staple in other incarnations. Colonists in New France compared the flavour of its meat to mutton. Boiled, peeled and roasted, the tail was considered a delicacy. The voyageurs were granted special permission from the Catholic Church to eat beaver tail on Friday, a logic which was apparently suggested by the beaver's ability to swim like a fish. Beaver pelts were also used as currency when hard coin of the realm was in scarce supply.

By 1635, beavers themselves were in short supply in the hunting grounds of the Huron. Finding new sources opened up the West. In 1794, the North-West Company built Fort Augustus near what is now Edmonton. One of the founders noted that beaver in the area "are said to be so numerous that the women and children kill them with sticks and hatchets."

Humpbacked and orange-toothed, the humble *castor* was well on its way to becoming a national symbol. In 1785, the Beaver Club of Montreal struck a medal featuring a tree-chomping beaver and the slogan "industry and perseverance." A drinking and carousing society for the lords of the fur trade, the Beaver Club members may have required a dram of their own motto "fortitude in distress," following the evening of September 17, 1809, when thirty-two guests reportedly downed sixty-two bottles of wine, twelve quarts of beer and an untold quantity of brandy and gin.

By suppressing both its heart rate and breathing, a beaver can travel ten city blocks in fifteen minutes — provided those city blocks are under water. Kits, born after a three-and-one-half month gestation period, are cared for by both parents for two years. The beaver is monogamous, a natural builder and to all intents and purposes, waterproof. Beaver dams create wetland havens for a community of birds and mammals. However, they can be fatal. Washout from a beaver dam in Northern Ontario derailed a train in 1922, killing two railway workers.

Overtrapping during the Depression led to critically low beaver stocks. Throughout the 1930s, the beaver-loving, Indian imposter known as Grey Owl made his anti-trapping epiphany into something of an industry, translating the antics of his companion beavers — McGinty, McGinnis, Jelly Roll and Rawhide — into book sales and federally funded movies. When he died in 1938, and was unmasked as English-born Archibald Belaney, the national parks department ended his conservation programs. Today, the beavers' greatest threat comes from human encroachment on their habitat.

One thing that is unlikely to change is the title of *The Beaver* magazine. Initiated by the Hudson's Bay Company in 1920 as a staff magazine, it evolved into a full-fledged magazine now published by Canada's National Historical Society and devoted to "Exploring Canada's History." When a forum over the notion of changing the title was initiated in 1996, furry opinion flew three to one against change. One reader described the title as "sacrosanct"; others threatened to cancel their subscriptions.

Canada's largest rodent — the strong, tireless and industrious beaver — was officially designated as our national emblem on March 24, 1975.

THE *ANNEDA* SOLUTION

SOLVING THE SCURRILOUS SCOURGE OF SCURVY

Stadacona (Quebec City), 1535 — One of the ugliest diseases to afflict early explorers also has one of the ugliest names ever to apply to a human condition. Scurvy was a scourge that plagued generations of seafarers. On his first trip around the Cape of Good Hope (1497-1499), Vasco da Gama lost half of his crew to the illness. In the New World, the ravages of scurvy might have stopped French explorer Jacques Cartier from venturing further than the present-day site of Quebec City had it not been for an Iroquois native named Domagaya.

Cartier and his crew of 110 spent the winter of 1535-1536 living aboard their icebound ships near an Iroquois village they called Stadacona. In his journals, Cartier wrote of "a pestilence" that ravaged the crew to such a degree that "on all our three ships there were not three men in good health." The symptoms he describes started with swelling in the legs which spread painfully into the upper body and the neck. In gruesome detail he notes "the flesh peeled off down to the roots of their teeth, while the latter almost all fell out in turn." Cartier tried psalm singing and prayer, but twenty-five crew members died that winter.

In the village, more than fifty natives also died, likely due to European diseases. The natives also suffered from scurvy, and Cartier observed the disease in Domagaya, who was the son of Iroquois chief Donnacona. He noted that one of Domagaya's knees had swollen "as big as the body of a two year old child" and his teeth had decayed to the gums. Less than two weeks later, Cartier saw Domagaya again. He was walking purposefully across the river ice in extreme cold and he appeared to be in perfect health. After some prompting, Cartier learned that Domagaya had healed himself by drinking a tea made from the ground bark, twigs and fronds of a tree the natives called *anneda* — probably eastern white cedar.

Within weeks, Cartier's crew was restored to health thanks to this simple remedy. The reason for the cure would remain a mystery for several centuries, but it was the vitamin C from the plant material that prompted such seemingly miraculous recovery. Dutifully, Cartier recorded the cure in his journals, with one critical omission — he failed to provide a description of the *anneda*.

In his early explorations, Samuel de Champlain also encountered problems with scurvy. While travelling in the area of the Kennebec River in 1605, he met a native chief whose name was pronounced *anneda*. "I was satisfied from the name that it was one of his tribe that had discovered the plant called *anneda*, which Jacques Cartier said was so powerful against the malady called scurvy," Champlain wrote, hopefully. However, the chief had no cure to offer.

Since *anneda* was the Iroquois word for spruce tree, supposition has it that the native Champlain encountered was from a different tribe. The introduction of farming to the colonies was finally instrumental in solving much of the scurvy problem.

In the far North, the Inuit had their own unique solution for scurvy — the Willow ptarmigan. A relative of the grouse, ptarmigan feed on the vitamin C-rich buds and twigs of the hardy dwarf willow bush. By eating the gizzards and intestines of the ptarmigan, scurvy could be avoided. In addition, the Inuit would eat partially digested seaweed found in the stomachs of seals and other sea mammals that they hunted. Unsavory, perhaps, but markedly preferable to the agonies of scurvy.

Solutions that native peoples had figured out centuries earlier continued to elude Europeans. During the eighteenth century, scurvy was responsible for more fatalities in the British navy than enemy action. In 1747, Scottish surgeon James Lind began studying the effects of diet on sailors with scurvy and found that feeding them oranges prompted dramatic results. Six years later, he published his findings in *A Treatise of the Scurvy*, recommending citrus fruit as a treatment and preventative. Although it took the British navy forty-two years to heed the advice, when lime juice was distributed as part of the regular ration to sailors on long sea voyages, scurvy was eliminated. From then on, British sailors had to live with the moniker "limey."

Unfortunately, ascorbic acid (vitamin C) is prone to oxidize over time and it deteriorates under temperature stress. This phenomenon haunted most nineteenth-century polar explorers and may have contributed to the loss of Sir John Franklin's third expedition in 1847.

Scurvy also afflicted soldiers during the First World War.

Dr. Murrough O'Brien from Dominion City, Manitoba, confronted the disease while serving as a medical officer to a railway unit in northwest Russia. He had the foresight to include lime juice in his supply order, but it had been dumped off in freezing temperatures and spoiled. In Donald Jack's authoritative Canadian medical history book, *Rogues, Rebels and Geniuses*, O'Brien admits that he found himself in "a bit of a pickle," until he remembered having read that potato peels were also effective in treating scurvy. His patients were Russians, but O'Brien did not feel he would have much success commandeering potatoes from the local authorities. "I took the easiest way out," he said. "I called in three or four of my best filchers and sent them after tubers. I got my potatoes, fed the patients skin scrapings, and the scurvy cleared up like magic." Such a simple solution to such an ugly scourge that is now all but forgotten.

EASIER SAID THAN DONE

MARC LESCARBOT SEARCHES FOR A HAVEN IN THE WILDERNESS

Port-Royal, Nova Scotia, 1606 — When Parisian lawyer Marc Lescarbot sailed into the Annapolis Basin after more than a month spent crossing the Atlantic he was filled with awe at the wooded, hilly beauty of the unexplored and unexploited wilderness. "So many folk are ill-off in this world," he wrote, "they could make their profit of this land if only they had a leader to bring them."

Lescarbot was an improbable adventurer, and in this period of the early settlement of New France neither his legal skills nor his knowledge of Greek, Latin and Hebrew were likely to ensure his survival. Instead, Lescarbot utilized his talent as a writer and poet to chronicle the unfolding of events. His *Histoire de la Nouvelle-France* has been praised as "one of the first great books in the history of Canada." It is a running narrative debunking certain myths that spread from the early writings of explorer Jacques Cartier, including tales of two-footed beasts, pygmies, people who never eat food and men without recta.

A poet at heart, Lescarbot wrote about everything from conspiracy to morality. He frequently visited with the Micmac native leaders and noted their customs and chants. Contrary to the opinions of others, he found the native societies to be largely more civilized and virtuous than those of the Europeans, although he lamented their ignorance of fine wines.

The colony at Port-Royal was barely a few years old when Lescarbot arrived but boredom had already set in. Founder Samuel de Champlain recognized that a diversion was required. During that glorious winter of 1606-1607 Champlain's "Order of Good Cheer" provided an evening of entertainment once a week, and the feasting that accompanied the festivities ensured that at least one nutritious meal was had by all. Fifteen colonists took turns being Grand Master of these social events, and each took pride in trying to outdo the others in matters of ceremonious presentation of huge dinners featuring wild game and seafood.

"Whatever our gourmands at home may think, we found as good cheer at Port Royal as they at their Rue Aux Ours in Paris, and that, too, at a cheaper rate!" declared Lescarbot, who was a member of the Order. He describes the scene as one of gaiety and pomp. "The chief steward, having prepared all sorts of things in the oven, walked with a napkin over his shoulder, the baton of office in his hand, the chain of Order around his neck, with everyone in the Order right behind him, each carrying his plate."

The Order ended in the spring of 1607 when the colony was disbanded and returned to France. But the experience of this freedom-filled wilderness had whetted Lescarbot's appetite and imagination. He returned to Port-Royal and continued to document, ruminate and compose rhymes of questionable merit. Life in the colony seemed to feed his creative instincts and, in one burst of enthusiasm, he orchestrated the first theatrical presentation in North America. His play, *Thèâtre de Neptune*, featured trumpets, cannon fire and a chorus of Tritons in bark canoes.

Lescarbot spent the final decades of his life in Switzerland and France, where he became a diplomat and returned to the practice of law. He maintained contact with the colony, but never returned.

Having romanced the wilderness, Lescarbot understood the challenges that the "freedom" of life in New France presented. "Many who are ignorant of navigation think that the establishment of a plantation in an unexplored country is an easy matter but it is much easier said than done," he noted. "In vain does one run and weary himself in search of havens wherein fate is kind."

The Fattest And The Rest

Women Are the Clue to Population

New France, 1663 — It was not always easy to convince settlers to come to this New World. Despite early attempts, by 1627 the population of New France was a lowly sixty-five souls. Early in the seventeeth century, settlement had been encouraged by providing land grants — feudal holdings — to groups with names like Company of One Hundred Associates and Company of Habitants. However, by 1663 when Louis XIV's reign as the "sun king" began, it was apparent that these attempts had fallen short, if not failed dismally.

As the saying goes, "it takes two to tango," and one of the problems of increasing the population had to do with the inadequate number of dancing partners. Estimates ranged as high as one woman of marriageable age for every six bachelors. The solution was simple — add women.

From 1653 to 1663 approximately eight hundred French women between the ages of twelve and forty-five received free passage to New France. Some were poor Parisian beggars and orphans, others were recruited from smaller centres such as Rouen. They were known as *les filles du roi* (the King's girls), and each arrived with a certificate from a priest attesting to her availability and moral character. Jean Talon, the first Intendant of the colony, indicated in a letter to the King's Minister Jean-Baptiste Colbert that he preferred that "those destined for this country be in no ways naturally deformed, and they have nothing exteriorly repulsive." Each young woman was accompanied by a dowry, sometimes including livestock, which also travelled on the bride ships.

Illustrations of the arrival of the *filles du roi* on the docks at Quebec often feature beautiful, apple-cheeked, wasp-waisted young women posed demurely in court dress pondering an assembly of elegant and politely eager suitors. Yet, after a crossing which often took at least two months, it is unlikely that anyone emerging from the ships smelled or looked anything close to rosy. The shipment of rouge was forbidden. In addition, manners in the colony were already at least one step removed from those in France, where urinating on the stairways of the Louvre was acceptable behaviour.

No doubt the scene on the docks was lacking in romantic idealism. In some accounts, "brides" were more or less cut out of the herd, with the fattest young women selected first on the principle that they might have the best chance of enduring a winter. Marriages were arranged quickly and within a few weeks an estimated 90 percent of each shipload of women had become wives.

There were rules to be followed after the marriage; however, they were scant and considerably incorrect by contemporary standards. For instance, a wife could only obtain a separation from her husband if he beat her with a stick that was thicker than his wrist. Farming was a subsistence occupation at best, but despite the hardships of the settlers' lives, wedlock had certain advantages. Intendant Talon denied bachelors the right to fish, hunt and trap. Unmarried women sixteen years of age and older and unmarried men of twenty and older were required to report every six months to explain their "situations."

Population became the goal of the state. In 1660, the King issued an Order in Council stating that any couple producing ten children would be eligible to receive a subsidy of 300 *livres* per child or 400 *livres* each if twelve or more births were recorded. This first "baby bonus" represented a healthy pension for parents and it produced results. A decade later, Intendant Talon reported that all of the "girls" sent the previous year were married "and almost all pregnant or mothers; a proof of the fecundity of this country." Between 1666 and 1672, the population more than doubled. The King granted a bonus to males twenty or younger and females sixteen or younger who married. Those who were not married by these ages saw their fathers *pay* a levy. Large families received the sanction of both the Church and the state. Talon returned to France, where he died in 1694 — a bachelor.

Other "bride ships" followed the pattern set by Louis XIV. During the gold rush in British Columbia the influx of thousands of miners caused a gaping disparity in the male-female ratio. In 1862, at least two shiploads of hopeful brides arrived in Victoria, B.C. They were organized at the request of the miners by the Columbia Emigrant Society, which included among its benefactors the Lord Mayor of London and the Bishop of Oxford.

The steamer *S.S. Tynemouth* carried the largest load — sixty-two women who were described as a "select bundle of crinolines" by the *British Colonist*, "varying from fourteen to an uncertain figure; a few are young widows who have seen better days." Commerce stopped on the September day when the women were greeted by the entire male population at the dock. Some were terrified by the sight of the men and some asked to leave immediately, but their reception was civil and dignified. Only one bride was claimed directly at the dock. The rest of the women walked to the Parliament buildings where they did their shipboard laundry together in pre-arranged tubs while all and sundry watched.

In time, almost all of the Victoria brides married, although it is said several chose to travel to the Cariboo gold fields to try their hand at mining or other more bawdy enterprise.

EÒIN A' CHUAN

NORMAN MACLEOD LEADS GAELIC "SEA BIRDS" ON A MASS MIGRATION

St. Ann's, Nova Scotia, 1851 — Visitors to the picturesque town of Waipu, north of Auckland in New Zealand, may be surprised to find that many of the residents call themselves "Nossies," after Nova Scotia. They are the descendants of a mass migration of Cape Bretonners who came to the North Island in the middle of the nineteeth century, led by the Reverend Norman MacLeod.

For thirty-two years, MacLeod ruled a colony of Scots at St. Ann's on Cape Breton Island. He came to settle there by accident. At thirty-seven, disillusioned with the Church of Scotland, he left his homeland and sailed for Pictou, Nova Scotia. By the time he landed, the charismatic but churchless preacher already had a following of shipmates who wanted to settle with him.

The lumber boomtown of Pictou was filled with

rum-runners and rowdy goings-on. MacLeod pronounced it "a land for shameless and daring wickedness." Instead of staying, he planned to take his followers to Ohio via the Mississippi River, and he built a ship which the Pictou natives jokingly called "the Ark."

On a trial run in the autumn of 1819, MacLeod and a small crew berthed the Ark in the harbour at St. Ann's. They found the environment hospitable, the water teeming with fish — they decided it would make a perfect place to settle. Cabins were constructed, along with seven small boats. The following spring, settlers from Pictou began relocating on the island. They were joined by other Scots and soon the colony took on the aspect of a Highland clan society, complete with Norman MacLeod as its ruler and latter-day biblical patriarch. He was called "Norman," his people were "Normanites" and the creed of his preaching was "Normanism."

MacLeod assumed absolute power, positioning himself as magistrate, teacher and arbitrator of all things. He had no friends, only worshippers, and his cruelty became the stuff of legend. Once he punished a boy for a petty theft by ordering that the tip of his ear be cut off. Later, it was discovered that the boy was not guilty, but his parents refused to take action in court because to do so would have been to "go against God."

In MacLeod's colony, the sanctity of the Sabbath was guarded with zeal. Roosters were covered with boxes on Saturday evenings so that they would not crow at dawn on Sunday. During the spring, buckets that filled with maple sap were spilled on Sunday so that no profit could be taken. Cooking was not allowed. Not so much as an apple could be picked. When MacLeod's wife Mary wore a ribboned bonnet to church instead of the requisite black, she was humiliated before the congregation. One of the only signs that MacLeod had any heart is reflected in the epitaph at the grave of a son who died in childhood. It reads: "Short spring; endless autumn."

MacLeod was quick to ban or discipline his followers for any slight, including signs of leadership ability, but he turned a blind eye to the misadventures of his brandy-smuggling sons. Still, hundreds of followers remained faithful, finding odd solace and unity in the rule of a tyrant. They built a church at St. Ann's that reportedly held as many as twelve hundred worshippers. Their sons and daughters attended school where classes were conducted in Gaelic. That linguistic and cultural tradition remains as one positive legacy of the MacLeod days. The Gaelic College of Celtic Arts and Crafts now stands on the site of the MacLeod settlement.

In 1848, disaster struck the self-contained community when a late spring frost destroyed the crops. By then, MacLeod had alienated any neighbourly sources of assistance. A petition to the government brought rations that staved off starvation, but the future looked bleak. Then, Norman got a letter that would change everything.

Years earlier, a black-sheep son named Donald had run away with the family ship, ending up in Australia where he became the editor of a newspaper in Adelaide. When the famine was at its worst, he sent a letter to his father describing the charms of "Down Under" and urging him to move the settlement to a continent half a world away.

Norman MacLeod was seventy years old at the time. His wife was over sixty and in poor health. Nevertheless, MacLeod's control over his "flock" was such that people who had barely heard of Australia prepared for a massive pilgrimage. By mid-summer the keel was laid for the first of six ships that would make the audacious voyage. Normanites were told Australia was the "destined land."

On October 28, 1851, the *Margaret* set sail with 140 passengers aboard, including 40 children. MacLeod sold the family home and property for $3,000 to purchase the sails and riggings for the ship, which was named after his vivacious youngest daughter. Five months later, they landed in Adelaide, only to find that the prodigal son, Donald, had moved on to Melbourne. They caught up with him a few months later, but found Melbourne wholly unattractive.

An Australian gold rush was on, and the booming swagger that abounded in the south Australian town made Pictou look tame. The Gaels of St. Ann's took shelter in a tent-city near Melbourne called Canvastown where an epidemic of typhoid claimed some of their number, including three of MacLeod's sons. When their money ran out, they were forced to sell the *Margaret*. Some of the settlers were caught up in the clutches of gold fever and left. It was not until a second ship from Cape Breton arrived that Norman MacLeod came up with the idea of moving to New Zealand.

Scots had established a colony in Dunedin on the South Island of New Zealand in 1847. Word of that success had reached as far as St. Ann's. In 1853, MacLeod wrote to the Governor of New Zealand, Sir George Grey, to request a block of land. He received an encouraging response. Although they were offered better land at Hawkes Bay, in 1853 the settlers chose a site on the eastern shore north of Auckland because the geography reminded them of Cape Breton. Eight hundred acres of land were purchased at the mouth of the Waipu River for £400 sterling. By 1860, more than 850 Normanites had made the exodus.

Again MacLeod established himself as the colony's overlord, but this time the settlers had outside influences. The Maori people taught them how to weave roofs and walls for their log cabins out of palm fronds. Semitropical forest was cleared and converted into fields where corn, pumpkins and melons flourished along with the Nova Scotians' staples: wheat and potatoes. When a reunion of the original settlers was held in 1903, the aged survivors bore names such as McKenzie, McKay, Campbell and McLean. They called themselves *Eòin A' Chuan*, Gaelic for "The Sea Birds."

Sam McPhee, director of the Celtic College at St. Ann's, is frank when he suggests that in contemporary terms, MacLeod's colony was virtually a cult. Just before he died in 1866, Norman MacLeod uttered his last Normanism to his followers, "Children, children, look to yourselves, the world is mad."

BY MANY NAMES SHALL YOU KNOW HIM

CROWFOOT — THE RELINQUISHING OF A BIRTHRIGHT

Blackfoot Crossing, Bow River, Alberta, September 1877 — In the culture of the Plains Indians in the late 1800s names were sacred to each family and were earned by acts of bravery and courage. When thirty-three-year-old *Isapo-muxika*, or Crow Indian's Big Foot, succeeded Three Suns as Chief of the Blackfoot in 1869 he had been variously known as Shot Close, Bear Ghost and Packs-a-Knife, each name a testament to acts that earned him the respect and reverence of his people.

By the age of twenty, Crowfoot (as he was called) had proven himself in nineteen separate battles and sustained a half-a-dozen wounds. But his appointment as chief was more a consequence of attrition than acclamation. A plague of smallpox, brought to the plains by white settlers, wiped out thousands upon thousands of native people, including most of Crowfoot's competition for the top job. Nothing — not his prowess with a knife nor his willingness to do battle nor his formidable constitution — could prepare Crowfoot for the devastation that was brought upon his people as a consequence of the white man's inexorable westward push.

Crowfoot's visage — the chiselled profile, the dark, weather-worn skin and piercing eyes — has made him the prototype for the perfect "Hollywood Indian." But posterity, at least, from many native perspectives, regard Crowfoot, with troubled ambivalence if not contempt. History books most often describe him as a great visionary and peacemaker.

Most of the great chiefs saw the futility of their circumstances — the European diseases to which their people had no resistance, the debilitating effects of the white man's whisky, the disappearance of the buffalo, the lethal power of the firearm. These phenomena ended native life as it had been known. But Crowfoot was unique in his seemingly infinite capacity to acquiesce and compromise. Because he was such a charismatic leader, the Blackfoot listened and obeyed Crowfoot almost until the day the Chief drew his last breath.

Instead of following Sitting Bull's imprecations to help him wipe out the North-West Mounted Police, and to capture more white women and more horses than the Blackfoot could ever imagine, Crowfoot balked. He took to heart Methodist Minister Reverend John McDougall's admonishments about whisky trading and stealing horses and allowed the Mounties to bring the white man's law and order, not only to the whisky peddlers, but also to the Blackfoot Confederacy. Crowfoot naively told McDougall, who may well have had the best of intentions, that the Minister's words made him glad. "In the coming of the Big Knives with their firewater and quick shooting guns, we are weak. We want peace. When you tell us about this strong force which will govern with good laws and treat the Indians the same as white men, you make us rejoice."

And rejoice they did, for about a week. By 1871, all of Canada's Plains Indians except the Blackfoot Confederacy had signed away their lands in six treaties. On September 22, 1877, for as far as the eye could see, four thousand Blackfoot, Piegan, Stoney, Blood and Sarcee erected a thousand teepees. The Mounties were there in force. Queen Victoria was represented in the person of Lieutenant-Governor David Laird of the Northwest Territories. He was known as "The Man Who Talks Straight."

Drums throbbed. There were games of daring and chance. The government distributed copious quantities of flour, sugar and tea. Over the five days it took to get all the relevant signatures — Crowfoot's was the last — Laird told the native leaders that the buffalo would soon be extinct. He promised them rights and privileges "for as long as the sun shines and the rivers run." There would be this, that and the other thing — money, cattle, ammunition, implements, seed — for each and every native person. Chiefs would get a medal, a flag and new clothes every three years.

When Crowfoot signed Treaty Number Seven, he granted 129,500 square kilometres (50,000 square miles) of arguably the richest land in Canada stretching between Cypress Hills, Alberta and the British Columbia border, in exchange for small change, a litany of Christian prayers and a series of empty promises. Crowfoot himself was already a wealthy and powerful man. At his peak he owned four hundred horses, had several aides on the payroll and serviced ten wives. Then he led his people to the oblivion of the reserve, where life was absolutely nothing like "The Man Who Talks Straight" had promised.

Now the white eyes could continue to wipe out the few

remaining buffalo with impunity. They could sell more whisky, more successfully, into a clearly defined, stationary and demoralized target market. Crowfoot's people began starving or drinking themselves to death. Government agents turned increasingly hostile. Young native leaders, including Crowfoot's adopted son Poundmaker, rallied and readied to do or die. As Blackfoot warriors, they demanded freedom and honour or death. Even Crowfoot began to doubt his own judgement and became increasingly unhappy and depressed.

In 1883, it became apparent that the tracks upon which the "iron horse" would run were going to be laid right through the Blackfoot reserve lands west of Medicine Hat. When the great Chief and Peacemaker himself became ill, the medicine men blamed the bilious, foul smoke streaming from the locomotives' stacks — clouds of which floated like fiendish apparitions over the limitless prairie horizons.

Neither the railway route nor the installation of the rails was part of the Treaty, nor had it been discussed. Convinced that Crowfoot's illness was derived from locomotive smoke and indignant over the lack of consultation about the railway — the warrior spirit — so much a part of the Blackfoot nature — rose as billowing smoke and threatened the incipient complacency. The Blackfoot started to tear up the rails under the cover of night as fast as the legions of steeves could spike them.

Sir William Van Horne of the Canadian Pacific Railway turned to a priest for help. He knew Crowfoot respected Father Albert Lacombe. Even while the young warriors armed themselves to resist the encroachment of railway gangs on their reserve lands, Father Lacombe conferred in deferential whispers with the ailing Crowfoot over copious amounts of tea and tobacco. Crowfoot was persuaded to call off the warriors.

Crowfoot's influential intervention allowed the CPR to push through Blackfoot land. Van Horne rewarded him with a lifetime railway pass, which the Chief remained inordinately proud of until the day he died. In 1885, five years before his death, he thwarted Poundmaker's plans, averting a bloodbath by successfully persuading the Blackfoot not to join with the Métis and Cree in the second Riel Rebellion.

"The white people are as thick as flies in summer time," the aging Blackfoot Chief told his people after returning from a government-sponsored trip to the East Coast. Crowfoot's final advice to rebellious young braves was for them to think about cattle, not buffalo.

The day Crowfoot died, a mourning nation shot the great Chief's favourite horse and buried its carcass with him, adding the rifle with which Crowfoot had once been so proficient. His people believed he would need both of them on the Greater Plains to which his spirit would travel and once again be free. A bronze cross at his gravesite identified Crowfoot as "Father of His People." Buried with him was a way of life thousands of years old. Nothing would ever be the same again.

WHO IS WHAT AND WHAT IS WHO

HOW A CANADIAN BEAR BECAME WINNIE THE POOH

White River, Ontario, 1914 — The Second Canadian Infantry Brigade was on its way east from Winnipeg to Quebec and the front lines of the First World War when army veterinarian Harry Colebourn bought the bear. It was a warm August day when the train carrying Prairie soldiers stopped for water and fuel at White River, a Northern Ontario lumber town. Colebourn spotted a trapper on the platform with a small black bear cub. As the story goes, the trapper had killed the cub's mother but the cub was so endearing he kept it. For twenty dollars, she was Harry's.

The bear became the soldiers' unofficial mascot. Colebourn named her "Winnipeg" after his hometown, but this was soon abbreviated to the endearing "Winnie." When the brigade was shipped overseas, the bear went with them. While the troops trained at Salisbury Plains outside of

London, she slept under Colebourn's cot and dutifully ate her rations from his hand.

In December of 1914, Colebourn was scheduled to transfer to the "Big Fight" in France, which he knew would be no place for a pet bear. He approached the London Zoo and released Winnie to their temporary custody.

Soon hundreds of children and adults were flocking to the zoo to see her. Although the zookeepers had to keep a wary eye on all of the other bears, they would not hesitate to enter Winnie's cage and give her a pat on the head. Children were given "bear-back" rides on her, and she delighted the crowds by fluffing her pillow and pulling her blanket over her great huge shoulders when she took a nap.

After the war ended, Captain Colebourn tried to retrieve his bear, but when he saw the incredible affection the British people had for her, he officially donated her to the zoo in January, 1919. Over the years, the Winnipeg veterinarian maintained a steady correspondence with the zoo and he was assured that Winnie was in good hands.

Colebourn's bear was not the only Canadian bear to find a home in the London Zoo. Records show that five of the species *ursus americanus* were placed at the zoo for safe-keeping by Canadian soldiers during a six-month period in 1914-15. However, there was something quite special about this Winnipeg bear. Not only was she the first, she was also a crowd-pleasing ham.

Among the many visitors who thrilled to the famous Canadian bear's antics were author Alan Alexander Milne and his young son Christopher Robin. In 1925, Milne was commissioned to write a Christmas story for the *London Evening News*. He wrote a story about a teddy bear named Edward who went "bump, bump, bump" down a staircase and ended up as that most treasured Bear of Very Little Brain — Winnie the Pooh.

Although golden in colour and anatomically incorrect in the illustrations drawn by E.H. Shepard, the storybook Winnie was modelled after the huge, black she-bear in the London Zoo who was famous for coming out to greet the crowds when a child so much as knocked on the Bear House door. "Pooh" was a word Milne's son is said to have used to show his disdain for a local swan that would not come when the child called.

Winnie the Pooh became a bestseller in 1926. Seventy years later, A.A. Milne's four volumes of stories about a boy and a bear who loves HUNNY, who has great adventures with his pals, Eeyore, Rabbit, Piglet, Kanga, and Owl remain a "warm and sunny spot" among the classics of children's literature.

Back in Winnipeg another little boy, Harry Colebourn's son Fred, grew up hearing real-life stories about his father's bear, Winnie. When Captain Colebourn died, Fred inherited six wartime diaries containing all of the bear facts. In 1987, through sheer coincidence, Fred learned that the London Zoo had contacted Calgary's Princess Patricia Light Infantry regarding "their" Winnie. History had become blurred after the lovable bear's death from old age in 1934. When sixty-year-old Christopher Robin Milne dedicated a bronze statue of his father's famous character in 1980, the plaque that accompanied it had attributed Winnie's origins to the wrong Canadian army company!

Fred Colebourn rushed to the breach, reclaiming his father's bear for the soldiers of the Second Infantry. In 1989, the citizenry of White River rallied to celebrate the birthplace of Winnie the Canadian Pooh in a festival that has become an annual event on the third weekend of August.

Saskatchewan artist Bill Epp created a sculpture of Captain Colebourn and his bear for the City of Winnipeg and in 1995 a duplicate was presented to the London Zoo.

As A.A. Milne wrote in the final lines of *The House at Pooh Corner*, "Wherever they go, and whatever happens to them on the way, in that enchanted place on the Top of the Forest, a little boy and a bear will always be playing."

And that is the story of Harry and his bear, Winnipeg.

An Alleluia In The Sky

The Crackling Candle Dragon
of the Northern Dawn

Northern Hemisphere, 1923 — To see the aurora borealis sweeping across the night sky like a shimmering curtain is to see a rare, sometimes unnerving natural phenomenon — but to *hear* the sound of light that appears to fall from the sky is even more remarkable. The few scientists who have experienced sound effects along with the visual pyrotechnics of the outer atmosphere's most vibrant visual display characterize it variously as a "crackling" and "hissing" or, more poetically, as the sound of "cellophane and steam." Clarence Chant, a professor at the University of Toronto who has been called "the father of Canadian astronomy," was watching a vivid display in 1923 when he became aware of its sound effects. He described it as "a subdued swishing sound, which grew more distinct as it approached and was loudest when the ribbon or belt of light was overhead."

Scientists are still trying to find an answer to the questions of why and how such sound might accompany the dance of the aurora. Magnetic storms, solar winds and sun spots have all been used to explain the electron phenomenon of the aurora, which was named after the Greek Goddess of the Dawn and has become more commonly hailed as the Northern Lights.

Popular science writer Terence Dickinson investigated the image of the aurora in early history and discovered that as early as 2200 BC the Chinese described the glowing, red image of a snake in the sky, which they called the "candle dragon." More than seventeen hundred years later, the Greek scholar Anaxagoras wrote that he had seen "in the heavens a fiery body of vast size, as if it had been a flaming cloud." In ancient Rome, Pliny the Elder saw the lights as "a flame in the sky, which seems to descend to the Earth on showers of blood." The Bible presents the phenomenon as "horsemen charging in mid-air clad in garments interwoven with gold." But those who live with the Northern Lights find few images of violence in their beauty. An Inuit legend suggests that the moving lights are caused by the spirits of dead friends and relatives playing a game of ball in the sky.

No two auroras are ever alike. Each one is the consequence of electrons and protons colliding with atmospheric atoms and molecules at least 56 kilometres (35 miles) above the earth's surface. Red and green colours are emitted at the highest altitudes, up to 970 kilometres (600 miles) from the ground, when atomic oxygen is released in a fixed wave of light. Ionized molecular nitrogen produces blue or reddish tinges, and sodium results in a display of yellow.

During intense displays, which usually occur in the spring and fall, pulsating curtains of light are swirled into clouds that sweep over the sky. The most brilliant and the rarest display is a coronal aurora in which even stars are obliterated by pulsing and flashing light that appears to stream in parallel lines from a magnetic zenith, although those lines never actually join.

The mighty dazzle is the result of electronically charged particles pumped out by the sun and manifest as solar winds that deflect around the earth's magnetosphere. Some of those particles become trapped in the magnetosphere and when enough of them accumulate, usually after a solar flare, they burst into an auroral ring of varying intensity and size that flows in a dome shape, centring on the geomagnetic North Pole, northwest of Hudson Bay.

More than a trillion watts of energy can be pumped into the rarefied upper atmosphere by an aurora. Geomagnetic storms have been known to cause surges in power lines. In 1982, the mining town of Buchan, Newfoundland, was left in darkness after a surge tripped a circuit breaker in the power grid. The phenomenon can also interfere with long distance radio communications. A spectacular aurora disrupted global telegraph communications in 1859. The sight alone can be disorienting. In 1939, fire brigades were dispatched to Windsor Castle in England when a red aurora was confused with a fire's glow.

Although the Northern Lights have been seen as far south as Singapore, the most spectacular view of them may be in the Northwest Territories. Today, tourists travel in droves to Yellowknife to sit in viewing stands and witness the sky show.

Two years before his death in 1977, Alberta-born artist William Kurelek created a series of paintings, drawings and observations of Inuit life that were published in his book *The Last of the Arctic*. Of the Northern Lights he wrote, "The only truly appropriate reaction seemed to be to whisper an Alleluia."

PART TWO

HEROES, HEROINES AND THE ODD VILLAIN

HOLDING THE FORT

THE HANGING JUDGE

CAPTAIN COURAGEOUS

NO NUDDER LIKE HIM

WHERE'S JOE'S BEEF?

LEAVE IT TO THE BEAVER

THE SITDOWNERS

TICKLING THE DRAGON'S TAIL

EKOKTOEGEE

HOLDING THE FORT

THE GLORIOUS INCLINATION OF MADELEINE DE VERCHÈRES

Fort Verchères, New France, 1692 — One of the most unusual recruiting posters of the Second World War featured a striking, stern-faced fourteen-year-old girl wearing a seventeeth-century dress and holding an ancient musket. According to the war department, the brunette vision standing on the shores of the St. Lawrence River "symbolizes the feminine heroism of Canada." Her name was Marie-Madeleine Jarret de Verchères.

There are many versions of the story of young Madeleine's heroic defence of her father's fort below Montreal on October 22, 1692. Madeleine herself added several embellishments and variations during her lifetime. There is no question that she was a young woman with a hearty survival instinct.

Madeleine was the fourth of twelve children. Her father, François Jarret, had served with the Régiment de Carignan, a 1,000-soldier force sent by France in 1665 to defend the settlers from attack by the Iroquois. After the Iroquois had been subdued by the French, the Régiment was disbanded. Two years later, in 1669, François married twelve-year-old Marie Perrot and they settled on a grant of land below Montreal called Verchères.

The family home became a fort while Madeleine was a toddler. The English and French were at war, and the British encouraged their Iroquois allies and trading partners to rekindle their attacks on French settlers. Isolated on the river, at least a day away from any military assistance, Fort Verchères was soon known as Château Dangereux. Attack was inevitable.

Madeleine was twelve when the Iroquois first stormed the stockade. Her thirty-three-year-old mother took command of a small force and drove them back with musket fire. Throughout 1690, French settlers waged their own brutal attacks on the English colonies and suffered the repercussions.

The summer of 1692 passed peacefully at Fort Verchères, which was well stocked with gunpowder and muskets. Madeleine's father left for military duty that fall and her mother felt the temper of the time was safe enough to leave her teenaged daughter "holding the fort," while she ventured to Montreal briefly for winter supplies.

From this point, the stories range freely. Some say Madeleine was gathering pumpkins when the attack began, others suggest she was on a wharf securing a water buoy when the bullets began to fly. According to the first rendition of her own story, Madeleine was running for the fort when a warrior grabbed her neckerchief, which she ripped off in the struggle to escape. Inside the fort, she rallied her meagre troops with the cry, "To arms! To arms!" In one version of her story, she discovered two cowering soldiers preparing to blow up the fort rather than risk capture, but she scolded them into taking their posts. In another, she dons a soldier's hat and takes to the ramparts herself — with an old man and two of her younger brothers firing muskets and creating the appearance of a much larger force.

Whatever diversions Madeleine created, they seemed to work on the Iroquois. When French and native allies arrived, they found only the dead in the field and the ragtag defenders of Fort Verchères under the leadership of a feisty slip of a girl.

The drama of her story sparked the interest of the French court, and when Madeleine's father died in 1700 his pension was transferred to her as a reward. By the standards of the day, she was a wealthy spinster when she married officer and seigneur Pierre-Thomas Tarieu de la Pérade in 1706. At fifty-four, Madeleine added to her legend by saving his life when he became involved in a brawl with two men.

Thirty years after the incident at Fort Verchères few eyewitnesses remained alive, so Madeleine retold her story in an apparent bid for a favour from France. Among other things, she added forty-five Iroquois to her evasive run to the fort and extended her single-handed defence to a full week rather than two days.

"Allow me to tell you that, like many men, I have feelings which incline me to glory," admitted the heroine of Verchères.

The Hanging Judge

Matthew Begbie — Have Gavel Will Travel

Victoria, British Columbia, 1856 — When English lawyer Matthew Baillie Begbie arrived in British Columbia to serve as the colony's first judge he appeared to be the epitome of an impressive jurist. His pointed mustache was waxed and his beard trimmed into a careful wedge. He had studied at Cambridge and was fluent in French and Italian. But the dashing aura — black cloak and wide-brimmed velvet hat — did not mean that the man who was to shape the law in British Columbia was necessarily well versed in the subject.

In fact, thirty-nine-year-old Begbie had failed to make much of a living in the courts of London. His brother had usurped the affections of his girlfriend and he was reduced to being a reporter for the *Law Times* when he was offered £800 a year to pronounce justice half a world away. Legal acumen was not the foremost qualification British colonial secretary Sir Edward Bulwer-Lytton had in mind when he ordered up his first judge. He wanted a man who could "truss a murderer and hang him from the nearest tree." Begbie was given fifteen constables to help him with the job.

Crime did not come to the court room during the Fraser River gold rush, so Begbie took his court to the criminals. The hard-riding judge kept a string of twelve horses. He carted his long judicial wig and scarlet robes with him and often meted out justice right at the crime scene. Trials were held in settlers' cabins, saloons, barns and even in open fields. When there was a scant pool of jurors, Begbie used transient Americans — which may have been an illegal practice, but it got the job done.

Sometimes the unorthodox judge even nipped crime in the bud. Arriving unexpectedly in Wild Horse Creek where a surly crew of armed miners had been fomenting a riot, he announced, "Boys, if there is a shooting in Kootenay, there will be a hanging in Kootenay." The miners named Begbie "the hanging judge." But delivering a death sentence was not something he undertook easily. Begbie often kept a chaplain at his side for moral support, and he was known to secretly lobby British Columbia Governor James Douglas to commute some sentences to life imprisonment. He had little use, however, for those who stood against him. Once he emptied a chamber pot over the heads of conspirators he overheard plotting to shoot him.

Begbie was no more charitable to some of his more obstinate juries. When a jury convicted a gambler of manslaughter rather than the "unmitigated, diabolical" crime of murder that he perceived, the judge reluctantly pronounced a life sentence. "Had the jury performed their duty I might now have the painful satisfaction of condemning you to death," he advised the prisoner in his shrill, nasal voice. "And you, gentlemen of the jury, are a pack of horse thieves, and permit me to say it would give me great pleasure to see you hanged, each and every one of you."

On another occasion, a jury acquitted an accused charged with sandbagging a companion in a Victoria barroom brawl. Begbie dismissed him saying, "You can go, and I devoutly hope the next man you sandbag will be one of the jury."

Single-handed, Begbie was able to establish law-abiding habits in a political climate that was under pressure from the envious eye of Manifest Destiny and its anti-British sentiments. During forty-six controversial years on the bench, his detractors never won a case against him. Defying popular opinion of the day, he defended the rights of Chinese immigrants. He threw out a law that forbade native feasts called potlatches because he thought them a good and harmless custom. When British Columbia entered Confederation in 1871, Begbie became its chief justice. Four years later he was knighted.

Following his death in 1894, Begbie's small estate was left to destitute citizens whom he had quietly supported for years, and for each of clergy friends there was $100 and a case of wine. At his request, his grave was marked with the simple epitaph, "Lord be merciful to me, a sinner."

CAPTAIN COURAGEOUS

WILLIAM JACKMAN FOLLOWS THE FAMILY CREED TO HEROISM

Spotted Islands, Labrador, 1867 — It is part of the lore of Newfoundland that at least one mariner has expired at the mere recollection of riding out a hurricane. It was a weather disturbance of just such memorable proportion that led the schooner *Sea Clipper* into a collision with another small schooner off the shores of Indian Tickle on the craggy coastline of Labrador. The other vessel was cut down, but all hands managed to clamber aboard the *Sea Clipper*, which proceeded down the coast toward Spotted Islands.

At the height of this storm — one of the worst recorded on the coast — a burly thirty-year-old named William Jackman, who was visiting nearby, decided to take a walk outside with his friend. Captain Jackman grew up in a family that was accustomed to the perils of the sea, but his hometown of Renews was considered to be part of the "south," and the sight of the storm may have piqued his curiosity. "I felt something tell me to take that course," he said later, leading to speculation that he was mystically guided.

At the headland, Jackman spotted the *Sea Clipper*. The overloaded schooner had been driven onto a reef, where the waves tore at her in the running sea and the gale precluded any notion of launching a rescue boat. To Jackman, who grew up swimming in the Atlantic, the solution was obvious. After instructing his companion to go back to the settlement and gather ropes and men, he stripped off his coat and boots and dove into the pounding surf.

Against all odds, he managed to swim the 200 metres to the *Sea Clipper*. Hoisting a man on his back, he made the return trip. Eleven souls had been rescued in this precarious manner before help arrived. The ropes must have been a welcome sight to the tiring Jackman, who tied the lifeline to his waist and went back for more. Twenty-six men had been returned from the sea and the *Sea Clipper* deck was empty when Jackman asked the assembled survivors if there were any others left to be dry-docked.

There was one, he was told. The only woman aboard had been too ill to bring up to the deck. She was thought to be dying, perhaps even dead, and certainly too weak to survive a saltwater rescue. Despite attempts to dissuade him, Jackman's gallant response is said to have been, "Living or dead, I will not leave her there." Back he went into the icy waters for the twenty-seventh journey.

He found the woman in the aft cabin of the wreck, too sick to move even though rising water threatened to engulf her. Strapping her to his own body, he managed to bring her safely to shore where she was wrapped in his coat, but the excursion proved too much for her. She died shortly after offering her thanks.

"Captain Will" soon became known as "Captain Courageous," and the Justice of the Peace for Labrador, Matthew Warren, was quick to sing the praises of his noble conduct. Bishop Thomas Mullock of St. John's took up the cause and a year later the Duke of Buckingham sent Jackman a medal for bravery from the Royal Humane Society. Although his countrymen wanted to celebrate his courage, Jackman was more introspective. He insisted that he was merely following the creed of his family, which demanded that one persevere until a task is completed. He gave the medal to his wife, Bridget, and never spoke of it again. His father, Captain Tom, illustrated the strength of the family creed when he told his son, "If you had not brought that woman ashore, I'd never have forgiven you."

Jackman spent the rest of his life commanding ships and men and confronting the dangers of the Labrador coast. The rigours of the rescue seemed to have tapped his great strength, however. When he died in 1877, just a few months shy of his fortieth birthday, all of the businesses in St. John's closed and flags flew at half-mast in honour of the hero of the wreck of the *Sea Clipper*.

NO NUDDER LIKE HIM

JERRY POTTS OF THE NORTH-WEST MOUNTED POLICE

Fort Whoop-Up, Alberta, 1874 — Imagine yourself in the middle of nowhere in the Canadian West, with a tight-lipped guide who carries neither map nor compass. Disoriented, perhaps concerned about the threat of attack by hostile elements, you ask the guide what he anticipates beyond the next hill. A little man with rounded shoulders and a stunted growth of whiskers, he eyes you narrowly and says, "Nudder hill." Such an experience became a familiar routine for members of the fledgling North-West Mounted Police (NWMP) when they travelled with Jerry Potts.

Potts was born in the United States at a fur trading post where his Scottish father clerked for the Hudson's Bay Company. His mother was a Blood Indian of the Blackfoot Confederacy. After Jerry's father was murdered in a case of mistaken identity, he grew up living variously with his mother's people and in white settlements.

As a young man, he fought in tribal wars and is said to have taken as many as nineteen scalps in one battle. His dress code was informal, and combined the influences of white and native cultures. Potts mixed a fedora hat with moccasins, and a bit of everything else in between. He was a superstitious man, always wearing the skin of a cat, which he believed would protect him from evil. He also refused to have a gun pellet removed from his left ear lobe because he had earned it in battle and thought it brought him good luck. He may have been right, since he died a few months after the pellet worked its way out of this lodging place of its own accord.

In the autumn of 1874, Potts was hired by Colonel James Macleod to lead the Mounties to Fort Whoop-Up, a bastion of whisky traders. As a guide, Potts was legendary. He was also said to be able to detect the smell of booze at a considerable distance, although he preferred to have the stuff close to him. Unfortunately, when Macleod and his troops arrived, the whisky runners had already fled — with their whisky.

Macleod tried to buy Fort Whoop-up to no avail. With winter fast approaching, Potts led the weary column of troops and horses to a spot on the Oldman River, where Macleod began immediate construction of the Force's first fort in the West.

For twenty-two years Jerry Potts guided the Mounties, earning a colourful reputation along the way. One corporal reported that he had "an unquenchable thirst which a camel might have envied. If he could not get it, he would take Jamaica ginger or essence of lemon, or Perry Davis' painkiller, or even red ink." After bouts of such drinking excess, Potts and his buddy, George Star, were said to try to trim their mustaches with their six-shooters, facing each other at twenty-five paces. Potts lived in a teepee outside Fort Macleod, where he had a combination of native wives, some say as many as four at one time, including two who were sisters.

Despite his personal quirks, Potts became a great asset to the Mounties. He spoke the languages of several tribes, and he proved instrumental in establishing trust between the Blackfoot Confederacy and the NWMP. On one occasion, after Blackfoot chiefs delivered lengthy speeches of welcome and gratitude to the Mounties, Potts translated by saying, "Dey damn glad you here." Brevity was his soul.

After twenty-two years of continuous service to the Mounties, Jerry Potts's hard-lived life ended when he succumbed to tuberculosis on July 14, 1896. Calling him "a type fast disappearing," the *Macleod Gazette* noted: "For years he stood between the police on one side and his natural friends the Indians on the other and his influence always made for peace. Jerry Potts is dead but his name lives and will live. 'Faithful and true' is the character he leaves behind him — the best monument of a valuable life."

WHERE'S JOE'S BEEF?

CHARLES MCKIERNAN — THE GENEROUS INNKEEPER

Montreal, 1878 — You did not have to look far to find the meat in some form or other at Joe Beef's Canteen on the south side of Montreal. In the 1870s and 1880s, it was the most flamboyant tavern in the city, and probably the only one that boasted a resident live buffalo in the cellar. Opposite an open pantry piled to the ceiling with loaves of bread, there was a black bear whose chain rattled when the inquisitive came too close for comfort. For good measure, there was a spare bear downstairs and two parrots held squawk on a perch over the bar.

An account recorded by Montreal historian Edgar Andrew Collard describes the patrons almost as though they were part of the motley but well-loved menagerie of animals. "There was not a good coat, or a hat in even modest repair in the company," he suggests. "Their garb was of the poorest, but it made no difference to their spirits — all hands were happy and contented." Beer cost five cents for a pint-and-a-half mug and it was largely consumed at the upstairs bar, since the pungent odour of the buffalo was harder to take than the screeching chatter of the birds. Next door there was the Rag Shop. All along the waterfront, saloons and cafés did as brisk a business as did the sixty or so churches on the sedate north side of Montreal.

Although colourful advertising promoted "Joe Beef of Montreal" as "the son of the People," the proprietor was actually a mustachioed Irishman named Charles McKiernan, whose wit ensured a steady clientele of "the homeless and the footloose of the world." McKiernan promoted the character Joe Beef as something of a poet-renegade in search only of "coin," with scant regard for the "Pope, Priest, Parson or King William of Boyne." His handbills suggested, "If you can walk or crawl, when you go on the spree, go and see Joe Beef of Montreal."

The city itself was a marvel of extremes. On one hand, Donald Smith, the president of the Bank of Montreal and the governor of the Hudson's Bay Company, was busy building a cut-stone baronial castle, complete with a ballroom, private art gallery and marble balconies. At the same time, workers were complaining to a Royal Commission on Labour Capital that wages for a sixty-hour work week averaged about seven dollars. The disparity did not elude Joe Beef.

In July, 1878, workers on the nearby Lachine Canal went on strike for a twenty-cents-a-day raise. Six years earlier, workers in Ontario and Quebec had launched the Nine-Hour Movement in an effort to reduce working hours from twelve to nine per day. In Lachine, ten-hour days were in force and the reward was eighty cents a day. To help them hold their course, Charles McKiernan supplied the striking workers with three thousand loaves of bread and five hundred gallons of soup for their families. Then he funded two delegations to present the workers' case in Ottawa.

When his wife died, the band from his regiment played the "Dead March" from *Saul* for the procession to the grave site at Mount Royal Cemetery. Her tombstone is marked with one of Joe Beef's impudent rhymes. On the way down the mountain, at the bereaved husband's request, the army band played a swinging rendition of "The Girl I Left Behind." The colourful innkeeper and philanthropist himself died in 1889 and the funeral was the largest ever seen in Montreal. Mourners lined the streets for blocks, and workers were given a half-day holiday.

Nobody in town had a beef with Joe Beef.

LEAVE IT TO THE BEAVER

MAX AITKEN MAKES HAY WHETHER OR NOT THE SUN SHINES

London, England, 1910 — A multi-millionaire before he was thirty, William Maxwell Aitken's furious, flamboyant omnipresence had a profound and lasting influence on Canadian commerce. A kind of Gorden Gecko, the amoral corporate raider portrayed in Oliver Stone's award-winning 1989 movie *Wall Street*, Aitken was a mergers and acquisitions man in the nascent Canadian market. His controversial transactions dog him, like an evil twin, even to this day.

A slight man with an impish face, "Max" seemed to come from nowhere. To the civilized world, Maple, Ontario, where he was born in 1879 to strict parents of Scottish-Presbyterian descent was nowhere. Not a particularly good student, by his own admission he was an impudent son.

Aitken's early years were a testament to the axiom that it's not so much what you know, but who. As a teenager in

Newcastle, New Brunswick, where his family moved shortly after he was born, Aitken had the remarkable good fortune to meet and befriend the considerably older R.B. Bennett, who was destined to become Prime Minister of Canada.

Aitken joined Bennett's law firm as a clerk, but soon dropped out. By twenty-one Max was truly nowhere. He had tried university, studied law, sold insurance, managed a bowling alley in Calgary and sold meat in Edmonton. He gambled and drank the proceeds of his labour.

Fate stepped up, in the person of John F. Stairs, a well-connected Halifax financier and politician whose acquaintance he made on a weekend fishing trip organized by R.B. Bennett. Stairs saw something in the youthful ne'er-do-well and staked Aitken as a stock promoter. Shortly thereafter, Stairs asked Aitken to amalgamate two small banks. When the youthful enthusiast made $10,000 in the process, his future was manifest. Aitken was soon managing a new investment house called Royal Securities.

In 1906, two years after his mentor's death, and under some kind of cloud, Aitken quit Royal Securities and moved to St. James Street in Montreal, then the financial heart of Canada. There he made a series of lightning fast, spectacular moves, including buying and selling Montreal Trust for a $200,000 profit. With this profit, he took over Royal Securities, facilitating a frenetic, profitable, international binge of acquisitions and mergers.

Aitkens bought and sold companies in the West Indies. He also started Calgary Power, but his most heavily rewarded talent was that of a "corporate bundler." He was to the 1920s and St. James Street what Michael Miliken was to the 1980s and Wall Street, except he was Miliken in reverse. Instead of "raiding" giant companies and dismantling them piece by piece, at an enormous profit until only a shell remained,

Aitken bundled smaller regional companies in the same business to create powerful corporations.

Aitken reasoned that only large Canadian corporations, shielded by tariff protection that he coerced his pal Prime Minister R.B. Bennett to instigate, could compete with giant American rivals. Aitken went about buying all the small companies in similar businesses he could find across Canada and amalgamating them.

By 1910, there was the widespread suspicion that Max Aitken had misappropriated more than $13 million in a 1909 merger which he engineered for Canada's three largest cement companies. Instead of the three he was asked to integrate, he merged thirteen cement companies into Canada Cement. Skillfully and arguably illegally, he excluded one of the original three which he knew to be debt-ridden and unprofitable. The case was eventually settled out of court, with Aitken making what to him by then was a nickel-and-dime rebate of $20,000 to the Bank of Montreal.

Even as this clamour over cement churned, Aitken was on to the next deal, buying Montreal Rolling Mills, Canada's leading steel-finishing plant. To keep the deal secret, he went to the London money market for the $4.2 million he needed to secure the plant.

He told his rivals he would not take a penny less than $5 million for the Rolling Mills facility and they tried squeezing him through the Canadian banks. To their horror, they discovered Aitken had outmanoevred them with off-shore financing. His price went up to $6 million, but now included one-third of the new, amalgamated Steel Co. of Canada. On the very day Stelco came into being, Aitken packed up whatever were his cares and woes, and moved to England. There Aitken met another New Brunswick expatriate, Conservative politician Andrew Bonar Law. Law invested $100,000 in a securities corporation Aitken established and doubled his money in two years, establishing a firm friendship.

Under Law's tutelage, Aitken became a Member of Parliament in 1910. Seven years later he was granted a peerage, moving into the House of Lords as the first Baron of Beaverbrook, a name he selected after a stream near his Canadian home. Three years later, Andrew Bonar Law became the first Canadian Prime Minister of England, but he was neither the first — nor the last — Prime Minister to be a confidante of Lord Beaverbrook. Kings and dictators sought "The Beaver" equally.

By the time Aitken was fifty, he had taken over and revitalized the London *Daily Express*, the *Evening Standard* and the *Sunday Express*, bought and sold Rolls-Royce, served in Lloyd George's and Winston Churchill's wartime Cabinets, helped oust Asquith and broken up the coalition between the Conservatives and the Lloyd George Liberals in 1922.

Embarrassingly, Beaverbrook steadfastly advocated a policy of appeasement with Nazi Germany and made many an approving remark about certain aspects of Nazism. He met with Stalin and advocated for a British alliance with Russia, jilted writer Rebecca West, befriended H.G. Wells, advised Rudyard Kipling about money, and generally became a master of shadow-boxing in the backrooms of international intrigue and power.

But there were those who saw him in a different light. Unlike Kipling, Churchill never took any of Beaverbrook's financial advice. Lady Churchill disliked Beaverbrook intensely, and called him a "microbe." She often scolded Sir Winston about this "bad influence." Churchill's successor, Labour Prime Minister Clement Attlee, said Beaverbrook was "the only evil man I ever met."

As Lord Beaverbrook, Aitken commissioned biographies about himself. For posterity, he wrote books which sycophants described as indispensable but were, in the words of historian Martin Gilbert, "never quite right."

Beaverbrook often governed his empire and many interests from a distance, for instance, from Villa Capponcina, his extravagant retreat in the south of France. In his hands, the telephone became a weapon. While he was chewing out his editors and barking instructions, his long-distance lackeys could often hear young women they disparagingly dubbed "Beaver's girls" giggling in the background. Beaverbrook set out to run England and the world through his newspapers. However, not one policy or issue he and his papers supported ever became public policy.

In 1947, he became Chancellor of the University of New Brunswick. He lavished approximately $20 million in gifts on his beloved Miramichi Valley. In Fredericton, he built skating rinks and libraries, an art gallery and a theatre — even a Beaverbrook Birdbath. Malcolm Muggeridge called it the "deliberate pre-humous creation of a shrine and a cult."

In spite of his philanthropies and his Zelig-like appearance in hundreds of photographs with legendary leaders, his real legacy seems to be a debatable lesson: that mass communications have little or no influence on opinion or behaviour. His daily newspapers appear to have set the precedent for their tabloid successors: contrary to being sources of reliable information and influence, they were really nothing more than entertainment.

H.G. Wells predicted that if he got the chance Lord Beaverbrook would try to merge heaven and hell. On May 25, in 1964, Lord Thomson of Fleet, a fellow Canadian-born press baron, threw a dinner party for Beaverbook's eighty-fifth birthday. Beaverbrook gave a speech in which he said that he had always been an apprentice and now it was time for him to become an apprentice once more. "Somewhere," he said, "sometime soon." He died on June 9, 1964, on his British estate.

The Sitdowners

Steve Brodie Leads a Transients' Strike

Vancouver, 1938 — Ironically, Steve Brodie's early exposure to politics would have been to hardline Conservatism and the lionizing of that triumvirate of earthly authority: God, King and Empire. But the lack of any godly grace in Brodie's life and the cruel Canadian prairie soon undermined the youthful Scot's naive beliefs.

The son of a preacher, Steve Brodie was born Robert Brodie in Edinburgh in 1912. "Steve" was a nickname he acquired later from his legion of rail-riding unemployed comrades in the Dirty Thirties in Canada. Brodie's relentless, never-say-die style reminded them of another Brodie named Steve — a working man's hero in the bleak, Depression landscape who plunged off the Brooklyn Bridge to win a bet.

Orphaned during the 1919-1920 influenza epidemic, Brodie came to Canada at age thirteen. Part of one of many mass orphan migrations organized by the Salvation Army, he walked off the boat onto an Eastern Ontario farm as an itinerant worker. Hearing there was work and a better life in the West, Brodie caught the last of the harvester excursion trains.

Reality was otherwise. The Canadian prairies had fallen prey to drought and desolation. When a Saskatchewan farmer introduced him to some socialist pamphlets, the seeds of revolt fell on fertile ground. Proudly, Brodie espoused his new views to his next employer. An Alberta rancher and no socialist, the man dumped the hapless farmhand on dead-of-winter Edmonton streets with ten dollars and the clothes on his back. That winter, like prairie permafrost, socialism sank deep into Brodie's soul.

Although he was a physical lightweight, Brodie had uncanny powers of persuasion with the single, unemployed drifters who travelled the rails, sharing the collective over-the-rainbow dream of steady work. Prime Minister R.B. Bennett told them they were lucky to get twenty cents a day building roads and levelling airfields. Brodie began to argue about the injustice of it all.

In the winter of 1933, Brodie rolled into the Rocky Mountains where he spent the time building fire trails and clearing beaver dams in a forestry camp near Banff, Alberta. In the early spring, he moved south to Vancouver, where the weather suited his clothes. He was not alone.

By 1938, the prosperous but provincial city of 246,000 had an unemployment rate of almost 30 percent. The city alone could not give relief to the thousands upon thousands of Steve Brodies sleeping fitfully under its viaducts and bridges. But there was no help and little sympathy from other quarters.

The transients were denounced by the Mayor and the

Prime Minister of Canada as dangerous, cold-blooded, Bolshevik agitators. They were deemed ruffians, who refused to be hungry and destitute with the quiet dignity reduced means traditionally commanded.

Brodie had joined the Communist Party and became an influential figure. Early in the summer of 1938, he and a select coterie of labour organizers plotted a mass demonstration. The idea was to organize a march and then surreptitiously, stealthily, with two thousand men, occupy three strategic buildings: the Vancouver Art Gallery, the Post Office and the Hotel Georgia. These stately edifices symbolized the civic, public and private interests that comprised the city's life-blood.

Nineteen years earlier, the Winnipeg Strike had been marred by extreme violence. In Brodie's view, although that strike had immobilized a city, the violence largely negated its point. Neither violence nor agitation were on the agenda for Vancouver. The sitdown was to be a peaceful demonstration.

Although RCMP infiltrators attempted to keep tabs on pending insurgencies, Brodie's scheme stayed under wraps. One minute — business as usual — the next, two thousand men squatted throughout three grand premises. When the local police chief, Billy Foster, requested Brodie take his men out, Brodie politely refused. Recognizing the seriousness of the situation and its inherent flaws, Foster immediately made arrangements with the Canadian Pacific Railway station for the use of its washrooms by the sitdowners.

Brodie's men occupied the large, marble-floored lobby of the Post Office. Once they regained their composure, postal clerks continued to transact business at their brass wickets. For the next thirty days, the public calmly threaded their way around and over Brodie and his increasingly bored band of sitdowners.

The peaceful demonstration display at the Hotel Georgia ended quickly. A group of city aldermen, concerned about the effect of bedraggled protesters on tourism, raised $500 and bought the men out. Brodie considered this a victory and an indication that the city accepted some responsibility for its population of transient unemployed. The money went to support the balance of the demonstration.

Meanwhile, the Art Gallery and the Post Office took on the semblance of a siege. Supportive women's organizations delivered hot meals. The YMCA opened its shower rooms, and a linen company provided towels. Local restaurants and churches offered free meals. A bakery donated bread and pies. A music store gave the men two radios, and a department store chipped in five hundred pairs of socks. There were even a few cots scattered among the bedrolls. And the protest had its own weekly newspaper. *The Sitdowner's Gazette* sold for donations ranging from ten cents to five dollars per copy. Its editorials were simple: the cure to the sitdowners' problems was work.

Brodie took time out to address a revival meeting, pleading the men's case from the pulpit and bringing tears to the congregation's eyes with his references to "that other Transient."

The Vancouver Sun complimented the protesters' "amazing restraint" and, after more than three weeks, Brodie's peaceful sitdown was beginning to attain its goal of shaming government into recognizing the men's demands for work and wages. However, it was naive in the extreme to expect that the authorities would ultimately respond with anything but disdain.

The buck was being furiously passed. From his cottage on Bowen Island, Vancouver Mayor George Miller disavowed responsibility for the demonstrators. From Victoria, the

Premier of the province, Duff Pattullo, said the sit-in was the concern of the Prime Minister, William Lyon Mackenzie King. King said the federal government was going to stick to its policy — and do nothing. But that was only a pose. Following orders that undoubtedly originated in Ottawa, RCMP Sergeant Bob Wilson lobbed the first Lake Erie Jumper — the popular moniker for tear gas — across the marble floor of the Post Office lobby. Hundreds of men, temporarily blinded by the gas, stunned by fear, leaped through the windows into the street where the Mounties and the city police began wailing on them mercilessly.

Brodie was the last man out. He wasn't difficult to identify in his trademark orange sweater. Sergeant Wilson and a group of Mounties began beating the defenceless Brodie in shifts. Finally, an RCMP constable stopped it. Brodie was staggering to his feet when a plainclothes detective with a rubber hose battered him back into the gutter.

Nearby, a photographer recorded the event. The brutality finally ended when the detective became self-conscious. Motionless, Brodie lay in the street, his orange sweater streaked with blood. Firefighters, who had been ordered to the site with their wagons, cursed the police for refusing to call an ambulance for the injured protestor. At great personal risk, a passing motorist picked Brodie up and delivered him to a hospital.

The beatings cost Brodie an eye, but otherwise he recovered. The single, transient unemployed men were given what they had been asking for all along — emergency relief, and jobs — five thousand of them, miraculously created by the provincial government in the name of public works. Briefly, Brodie became as heroic a figure as his bridge-jumping namesake.

The RCMP and the city police — under savage criticism

— quarrelled volubly over whose brutality had turned a peaceful demonstration into an ugly riot. Daily newspapers placed the blame "squarely on the institution of the government in Canada." Much later, there were some questions in the House of Commons.

During the Second World War, Sergeant Bob Wilson found work infiltrating various ethnic groups in British Columbia and then ratting them out to an increasingly paranoid government. Brodie served in the merchant marine. In peacetime, he worked on federal weather ships. Still later, he found gainful employment at the Victoria shipyards.

One day, Brodie raised a fuss in a government office over some injustice and found himself, twenty-nine years after his fifteen minutes of fame, unknown, unsung and unemployed — again.

TICKLING THE DRAGON'S TAIL

LOUIS SLOTIN'S SUPERCRITICAL SACRIFICE

Los Alamos, New Mexico, 1946 — In the time it took for a screwdriver to slip from his right hand, Louis Slotin was dealt a death sentence. The Winnipeg-born physicist was demonstrating the manipulation of two halves of a beryllium-coated sphere which formed the guts of an atomic bomb. The screwdriver that separated them was the only thing preventing a deadly chain reaction known as supercritical. Slotin called this exercise "tickling the dragon's tail."

When the simple tool dropped at 3:20 p.m. on May 21, 1946, a hot blue flash of gamma and neutron radiation filled the top-secret laboratory in Los Alamos, New Mexico. A Geiger counter clicked hysterically. Without pausing, Slotin leaned forward over the globes and pulled them apart with his bare hands. In that selfless instant, Slotin was exposed to almost one thousand rads of radiation, a lethal amount. His heroism served to shield seven observers. Although they received far lower doses, three out of the seven died years later from complications that may have been linked to their exposure.

Slotin vomited almost as soon as he left the building. He had a burning sensation in his left hand and a sour taste in his mouth. Before rushing to the hospital, the group reassembled in the laboratory, methodically plotting a diagram to determine where each of them had been standing at the time of the accident. The moment must have seemed surreal in its horror. "Everyone was wondering who had gotten most of the radiation," recalled security guard Patrick Cleary.

Nine days later, after suffering the agonies of radiation-induced trauma, Louis Slotin was dead. Citations honoured his bravery, but at his funeral in Winnipeg where three thousand mourners gathered outside his parents' home, Rabbi S. Frank recalled him as "one of the most brilliant scholars to ever come out of this city."

Louis had entered the University of Manitoba at the age of sixteen. After receiving his Masters of Science degree with Gold Medals in chemistry and physics, he pursued his studies of biochemistry in England. With his doctorate in hand, he returned to Canada in 1937, but he was unable to secure a job at the National Research Council, raising suggestions in later years that administrative anti-Semitism may have dogged his application. Instead, Dr. Slotin was welcomed at the University of Chicago, where he was introduced to nuclear physics by pioneer atomic chemist William Harkins. Although Harkins's research was underfunded, Slotin's work with an atom-smashing cyclotron attracted the attention of the Manhattan Engineer District — the cover name for America's atomic bomb program.

Slotin soon developed a reputation for skill in assembling the firing mechanism for the A-bomb. It was the product of his handiwork — a bomb code-named "Trinity"

— that demonstrated the awesome destructive powers of nuclear knowledge for the first time when it was detonated in the New Mexico desert on July 16, 1945. Three weeks later, a bomb code-named "Little Boy" was dropped on Hiroshima; another followed three days later on Nagasaki.

Working on the atomic bomb presented a myriad of ethical dilemmas that would haunt many of the scientists at the nuclear research laboratory in Los Alamos. Two months before his accident, Slotin explained in a letter to a colleague, "I have become involved in Navy tests, much to my disgust. The reason for this is that I am one of the few people left here who are experienced bomb putter-togeth-eres." To his father, Slotin reportedly explained his involvement with weapons of destruction by simply stat-ing, "We had to get it before the Germans."

Colleagues admitted they were aware that Slotin's pro-cedures were unsafe, but noted that "he would always insist upon taking the greatest risk himself." Critics cited the whole affair as a scandal and secrecy shrouded the accident for decades.

The dangerous practice of conducting hands-on assem-bly ended following Slotin's accident. Remote control systems were constructed to separate the operating crew from their equipment by the space of approximately four football fields. If the dragon's tail was going to be tickled, it would be at a respectful distance.

EKOKTOEGEE

JUDGE SISSONS LISTENS TO THE INUIT

Yellowknife, Northwest Territories, 1955 — When the police arrived, they found a gun within arm's reach of the lifeless body of Allan Kaotak's father. Closer examination revealed a piece of twine tied to the trigger.

Allan Kaotak, an Inuit from Cambridge Bay on Victoria Island, explained the string. He said he had done what any dutiful, loving son would do. He had rigged the gun to help his ailing, aged father commit suicide.

The Royal Canadian Mounted Police charged Kaotak with murder. His Yellowknife trial took place half a territory away from Cambridge Bay.

The Crown argued that Kaotak had murdered his father after a dispute over an arranged marriage. The defence said it was assisted suicide and assisted suicide was *de rigueur* in Inuit culture.

This dramatic conflict of culture, custom and law was the

first case presented to John Howard (Jack) Sissons, the first judge of the Territorial Court of the Northwest Territories.

Sissons was born in Orillia, Ontario in 1892. A survivor of childhood polio, he walked with a limp for the rest of his life. He grew up living on the grounds of the local mental asylum where his father was chief superintendent. On his mother's side, Sissons was related to the Scottish explorer David Livingstone. Stories about Livingstone's adventures in Africa shaped Jack's youth.

In his memoirs, *Judge of the Far North*, Sissons wrote that it was Livingstone's "hatred of injustice, his anger at the abuse of colonial power ... his understanding and affection for the native African and his respect for their natural human rights" that held sway over him. This sway led to landmark decisions in the North.

Sissons graduated from Queen's University in 1917 and moved to Alberta where he studied law. In 1921, he opened a practice in Grande Prairie. In 1929 he married an Irish visitor, Frances Johnson. They had two children, a son Neil and a daughter Frances.

With the help of a Métis campaign manager, the staunchly Liberal Sissons won the Peace River seat in 1940. As a Member of Parliament, Sissons sought and won inclusion for the seven hundred Métis of the Lesser Slave Lake area in treaty arbitration. Because they were considered half-breeds by blood Indians and ignored by Ottawa, this was quite a victory. Defeated in 1945, the following year Sissons was named to the district court in southern Alberta by Prime Minister Mackenzie King.

During his years as a judge in Alberta, Sissons earned a reputation that often placed him at odds with bureaucracy. Critics called him unorthodox, cantankerous and "a stubborn old coot." Sissons was sixty-three and had never been north of the sixtieth parallel when he accepted the appointment to the Territorial bench.

Uncharacteristically for appointed officials of the day, Sissons decided to research the culture of the people he would judge. In the case of Allan Kaotak, he discovered that suicide was an accepted Inuit solution for old age, infirmity and chronic illness. It was also considered a relative's duty to assist the afflicted.

Out of the gate, Sissons arranged that six non-native jurors were replaced by Inuit from Cambridge Bay. The jury took only twenty minutes to find Kaotak not guilty.

"Justice to every man's door" became Sissons's credo. "The flying judge" took his court on the road over a land mass that stretched from the Yukon to the eastern bluffs of Baffin Island. For eleven years, travelling by single-engine Otter aircraft and dogsled, he meted out justice in the landscape of the accused. Understanding that justice had to be seen to be done, the media-savvy judge often invited reporters to accompany him on his circuit. Cases were tried in kitchens, cockpits and igloos, with Sissons in full robes and the dignity of justice maintained.

In 1958, Sissons presided over a trial involving murder, child abandonment and negligent death. *Regina vs. Kikkik* was a tabloid journalist's dream and received a great deal of coverage in the United States, as well as Canada.

Kikkik, an Inuit woman, was accused of murder and abandoning her children, causing one of them to die unnecessarily. In the Chief Justice's opinion, the "bright boys in Ottawa" — a Sissonsism for the mandarins in the nation's capital — were the ones who were most responsible.

Amid questionable reports that the caribou herds were dwindling in the interior barren lands, the Department of Indian and Northern Affairs decided to move the Ihalmiut

Inuit from the interior to the coast of Hudson Bay.

On their way to Eskimo Point on Hudson Bay, Kikkik, her husband Hallow, her five children and her half-brother Ootuk, became stranded in a blizzard several days' travel from an outpost at Padley. Hallow left the igloo to ice-fish but was shot and killed on the ice by Ootuk, who wrongly believed that his travelling companions were withholding food.

When Ootuk returned, Kikkik sensed something was wrong because he refused to surrender the gun that had been loaned to him. A struggle ensued and shots were fired. Unaware that Hallow was dead, Kikkik restrained Ootuk and sent her daughter Ailoyoak to get Hallow. When the daughter returned with news of Hallow's murder, Kikkik tried to stab Ootuk but her knife was too dull. She got another knife from her daughter and fatally stabbed Ootuk in the heart.

In the following days, Kikkik set out with her children to try to reach Padley despite desperately cold temperatures. They met some relatives who were also starving, but after a few days of travel Kikkik and her children were unable to keep up. One night she and her children remained behind, sleeping in the open. When they finally caught up with the relatives, Kikkik was told to stay in the igloo they had built and wait for help. After five days without food, Kikkik and her family once again set out for the outpost at Padley.

Realizing that she was not strong enough to manage all five children, Kikkik left her two youngest behind, wrapped in caribou hide in a snow house she built using a frying pan as a tool. Later that day, a search plane found Kikkik and her three remaining children. Kikkik was afraid and she told the authorities she thought the two children she had left behind were dead. The following day the RCMP found the infants — only one of them had survived.

At the beginning of the trial, Sissons explained to the jury that Kikkik was "a woman of a Stone Age society," and that if justice was to be served, everyone had to try and understand her behaviour in that context. A jury of four whites and two Inuit acquitted Kikkik on all charges.

Judge Sissons presided over many precedent-setting cases which dramatically put Inuit culture at odds with the white man's mores and law. He recognized the legitimacy of Inuit marriages, which the Department of Indian and Northern Affairs characterized as unlawful due to lack of formal registration. "White Christendom does not have a monopoly on virtue," he said. In accordance with native treaties, he defended aboriginal hunting rights. Sissons asserted the validity of Inuit customs, decrying Ottawa's "colonial bureaucracy," which he once described as "seeking to control everything but the Northern Lights."

To the Inuit, Chief Justice Sissons was known as *Ekoktoegee* — "He Who Listens." To Sissons, the Inuit were "the people par excellence." He died in 1969, two years after the Northwest Territories became self-governing.

PART THREE

HERSTORY

A ROYAL CANADIAN LOVE STORY

NO SEX PLEASE, WE'RE DOCTORS

A SPY FOR THE YANKEES

THE RIGHT TO BE BEAUTIFUL

FOR HOME AND COUNTRY

OUR LADY OF THE SOURDOUGH

"FOR THERE SHALL BE A PERFORMANCE"

A ROYAL CANADIAN LOVE STORY

MADAME ST. LAURENT AND HER PRINCE IN HALIFAX

Halifax, 1794 — Although she never saw it, the heart-shaped pond that ripples like a permanent valentine on the grounds of Prince's Lodge overlooking Bedford Basin is commonly known as Julie's Pond. There is also a street called Julie's Walk in her honour. "Julie" was a woman of many names — the longest of which was Alphonsine Julie Thérèsa Bernardine de St. Laurent de Montgenêt, Baronne de Fortisson. Most often she is called Madame St. Laurent, and for almost three decades she was known to be the mistress of Edward, Duke of Kent, fourth son of King George III — and the man who fathered Queen Victoria. Edward was twenty-seven when he arrived in Halifax to assume command of the forces of Nova Scotia. His mistress was thirty-four.

They had met three years earlier in Gibraltar, where Edward was cooling his heels after a scandal involving a French actress and an illegitimate child, not to mention his considerable debts. She was French from a bourgeois family in Besançon, and she had a history of romantic entanglements. For his part, the Prince was lonely. He had written his brother, the Prince of Wales, that he was "looking for a companion, not a whore." When Madame St. Laurent arrived in his life, he wrote to another of his brothers that she met his "every qualification ... good temper, no small degree of cleverness, and above all, a pretty face and a handsome person." In 1791, they sailed to Canada together, settling first in Quebec.

In her definitive account of the romance, *The Prince and His Lady*, author Mollie Gillen notes: "The pretty girl from Besançon would live all her days with her prince in a strange sort of twilight, flitting like an almost invisible woman in and out of personal letters but never appearing in official reports or the public press." One of the few public records that identifies Madame St. Laurent as "Julie" is a 1792 Quebec baptismal record showing that the Prince and his consort were godparents to the son of their friends Ignace-Louis and Catherine de Salaberry. In the margin of the document, near Madame's exhaustive full name, someone wrote "Julie."

While Prince Edward busied himself with his regiment, Madame St. Laurent tended to matters of the household. She served as a discreet hostess, removed from ceremonial duties and public functions. Still, word of her existence caused tongues to wag. In England, the *Morning Chronicle* of April 25, 1793, reported: "An illustrious Prince, it is said, has formed an attachment with a beautiful Marseilloise, who is highly spoken of for mental as well as personal accomplishments. She is one of the *rank* and *file* in the garrison of Montreal."

During the American War of Independence some forty thousand Loyalists fled to British territory, with the largest preponderance settling in the area of Nova Scotia. Through their enterprise, the colony flourished. It was also no stranger to British Royal Princes and their romantic proclivities.

Beginning in 1786, William, the Prince of Wales, spent three summers in Halifax where he was a naval captain. William was said to have a romantic relationship with Frances Wentworth, a married woman of ambitious character. Her husband John was appointed as Nova Scotia's governor when the Prince returned to England. The Wentworths were among the first to welcome Prince Edward and Madame St. Laurent when they arrived in 1794, and it was their country home that would become Prince's Lodge.

The main residence was an Italianate villa with large windows that looked out over the sheltered harbour of Bedford Basin. Prince Edward immediately set to work on improvements to the property, transforming the rugged bedrock landscape into gardens suitable to an English estate. An artificial lake was created by diverting a stream — but its heart-shape would be crafted much later, in celebration of visits by the Prince's grandsons Edward and Arthur. On a rise, he built a wooden rotunda known as the "Round House" which served as a music room.

The relationship between Madame St. Laurent and her Prince became quite public. The couple delighted in attending the theatre. On one occasion, the *Halifax Chronicle* published a flowery rhyming verse that rhapsodized about Madame's "bewitching eyes" and "fragrant lips." Although some straitlaced members of society made it clear that the Prince's courtesan was not welcome in their company, Madame St. Laurent accepted the rebuffs with quiet grace. In a private letter to the Undersecretary of State in London, Governor Wentworth noted, "She is an elegant, well bred, pleasing sensible woman, far beyond most.... I never yet saw a woman of such intrepid fortitude yet possessing the finest temper and refined manners."

The Prince was never thoroughly satisfied with colonial life, or with the climate. He worked hard at fortification projects, dabbled in telegraphy experiments and continually shaped his troops, always hoping that his efforts would earn him a transfer. There were occasional respites from what he described as "the dreariness of Nova Scotia," such as his trip with Madame back to England for his investiture as the Duke of Kent. However, it was an injury suffered during a horseback riding accident that proved to be his ticket out.

Madame accompanied her Duke on subsequent travels to England, Gibraltar, Belgium and France. As they aged, the relationship changed, but the friendship, affection and trust endured.

When Princess Charlotte, the daughter of the Prince Regent died in childbirth, there was a scramble to marry the aging bachelor princes and produce heirs. On May 8, 1818, Edward set out the terms of a security fund he had established for Madame St. Laurent, hoping this would be "proof of how dear she will always be to me ... to my last breath, as a true and faithful friend in every eventuality." A long-time friend from Nova Scotia, James Putnam, was one of the trustees. Shortly afterward, Edward married a German princess. Their daughter, Alexandrina Victoria, was born the following year.

Even as a newlywed, the Duke maintained a correspondence with his former mistress, whom he knew was stricken with grief. It is often reported that Madame St. Laurent ended up in a convent. In fact, she appears to have stayed in France, uncloistered and close to her family.

The Duke died from complications caused by a persistent cold in 1820. Immediately upon his death, the Duchess of Kent wrote a letter to the mistress she knew would also be grieving. The two women never met; however, correspondence from Madame St. Laurent to her lover's widow is said to have moved the Duchess deeply.

The woman Haligonians called Julie was three weeks shy of her seventieth birthday when she died in Paris in 1830. At her side was a friend who had visited Madame and Edward in happier times at Prince's Lodge. He was Louis-Phillipe, the new King of France.

No Sex Please, We're Doctors

The Posthumous Unmasking of Dr. Barry

Montreal, 1857 — The first woman to work as a doctor in Canada caused a sensation when she drove through the streets of Montreal in 1857 with her black manservant and small white dog in a red sleigh complete with uniformed footman and coachman. She wore a musk ox fur coat and favoured hats with plumes. Her skin was smooth and red hair framed a tiny face, dominated by large expressive eyes and a proboscis of considerable dimension. Petite and trim, she tended to strut — even into her sixties — although sometimes her movements seemed awkward since her sword clanked perilously close to the ground. She was the chief military doctor for all of Upper and Lower Canada in an era that did not permit the nation's women to study medicine, but her real name remains a mystery — to the men who served under her she was known as Dr. James Barry.

The "great revelation" of Dr. Barry's sexuality was made

known only after a staff surgeon had recorded her as a male on her death certificate in 1865. A char woman who was preparing the body for burial determined the truth. She began spreading gossip about Dr. Barry's bosom and abdominal stretch marks, which suggested that "he" had once given birth.

To explain the oversight, the doctor in charge began insisting that Barry was a hermaphrodite, but no autopsy was ever performed to support this conjecture. As medical biographer Carlotta Hacker points out in her book *The Indomitable Lady Doctors*, the only reasonable explanation for Dr. Barry's masquerade is that being a male was the only way any woman of the period could practise medicine.

James Miranda Stuart Barry's parentage is also a mystery. She is believed to have been the niece of artist James Barry, a freewheeling intellect who taught at London's Royal Academy and followed the vision of English feminist Mary Wollstonecraft, author of *A Vindication of the Rights of Women*. The incorporation of the feminine appellation "Miranda" related to a family friend, General de Francisco de Miranda.

When Barry entered Edinburgh University in 1809, her masculine identity was firmly established since the university would not have considered accepting a female student in any area of study, let alone medicine. Her chaperone for that first year in Scotland was a Mrs. Bulkeley and Bulkeley is believed to have been Dr. Barry's true surname. Speculation aside, the cross-gendered doctor's origins may never be known since she was as secretive about her past as she was her undergarments.

Certainly, Dr. Barry's sexuality had nothing to do with her medical abilities. After graduation from Edinburgh University, she rose quickly through British army medical ranks and served as Assistant Surgeon to the Colonial Inspector and Physician to the Governor's Household during her first overseas posting in Cape Town, South Africa. While there she performed one of the first Caesarian operations in which both mother and child survived. She is also said to have saved the life of the typhus-stricken Governor, which led them to become close friends. In fact, the friendship between the two men caused gossip. When George Thomas Keppel, then Lord Abelmarle, first met the Governor's medical advisor he wrote, "There was a certain effeminacy in his manner, which he seemed to be always striving to overcome." Some comments were a bit too much for Dr. Barry to stand for and demanded "his" participation in at least one duel.

As much as Barry succeeded in the art of disguise, she failed in the dance of politics, outraging the army hierarchy with her outspoken letters and demands. Barry's goals, however, were irrefutably in support of better treatment for the everyday soldier, and she was acknowledged as an excellent surgeon. She received consistent promotions, serving in the West Indies, Corfu and Crimea, before embarking on her reform of Canadian barracks and dietary conditions. Among other things, she insisted that feathers replace the straw in pillows. Although she maintained a vegetarian regime, she commanded that the soldiers' diet be varied and include "a cheering change of a roast instead of eternal boiled beef and soup." She also insisted on private rooms for conjugal visits, a notion that apparently had eluded generations of army doctors before her.

Following the revelation of her sex, numerous attempts were made to discredit Dr. Barry's achievements. The scandal was shocking enough, but the notion that a woman had functioned admirably and professionally in the male sanctum of medicine was intolerable to Victorian sensibilities.

Still, the troops Dr. Barry tended in Canada must have appreciated her contribution to a soldier's well-being.

Eighteen years after Dr. Barry's posthumous unmasking, Dr. Augusta Stowe became the first woman to graduate from a Canadian medical school. Other Canadian women, including Augusta's mother, Emily, had already paved the way for the acceptance of women doctors by taking their degrees in the United States where universities were more liberal in attitude. Dr. Stowe was under no pressure to keep her sex a secret. She married classmate John Benjamin Gullen while the ink on her diploma was still fresh.

A SPY FOR THE YANKEES

SARAH EMMA EDMONDS CROSSES MORE THAN ENEMY LINES

Moncton, New Brunswick, 1858 — Sarah Emma Edmonds was more than likely not the sort of young woman to wear fancy hats. At the age of seventeen, however, she and a friend established a ladies' hat shop in Moncton. Known as "Emma," Edmonds was raised on a farm in the bush near Magundy. She was always a bit of a tomboy, able to out-ride and out-shoot her peers and her siblings. It was a hard-working lifestyle, and Edmonds's father was known to be something of a vengeful tyrant. When she was barely a teenager, he tried to force her into marrying an elderly farmer. With the help of her mother she ran away, finding anonymity in Moncton as a milliner's apprentice.

By 1858, she was managing her own business, but she was constantly worried that her father would find her. He did. Before he could take her back to the bush, she moved to Saint John. There she took on the first of many disguises, cutting her hair, changing her wardrobe and adopting the persona of a young man, Franklin Thompson. From that time forward, Edmonds became a skilled practioner of gender deception.

A New Brunswick newspaper carried an advertisment from an American publisher who was looking for an agent to travel the countryside selling Bibles and other religious books. It was a job that apparently suited "Franklin" quite well. "Mr. Thompson" ended up working at the head office in Hartford, Connecticut, before moving to Flint, Michigan.

When the American Civil War broke out in 1861, twenty-year-old Edmonds was one of thousands of Canadians from coast to coast who enlisted. Canadian sentiment ran so high that some Canadians, such as the all-black Victoria Pioneer Rifle Company of Victoria on Vancouver Island, formed their own units. All Edmonds had to do was convince the medical examiner at Company F of the Second Michigan Regiment that she was a male, something she had years of practice in doing.

"Private Thompson" volunteered to work at the regimental hospital, an unpopular assignment since it meant exposure to epidemics of measles, mumps and chicken pox, which killed many Union soldiers before they even saw battle. Later she joined in combat herself, fighting at the battle of Bull Run and other major engagements.

She then joined the secret service, a move her memoirs suggest was simply to "serve her adopted country." To avoid suspicion in the ranks, she was appointed as the regimental mail carrier. This ruse explained her absence from the regiment and allowed her to courier messages to the high-ranking officers who had selected her because she was such a capable young "man." Her first mission as a spy was in

1863. Using what she described as "chemicals," she darkened her face and other visible extremities. Wearing a black wig and the clothing of a male slave, she infiltrated a Confederate fort at Yorktown, Virginia, and collected information about troop strength and artillery stocks. This disguise was used with success on several other such missions. Alternatively, she would pose as an escaped female slave, and even as an Irish peddler woman, complete with an accent she recalled from her childhood in New Brunswick.

A chance encounter with a Confederate officer, who thought he recognized her as Franklin Thompson, led Edmonds to an even more dangerous assignment in counterespionage. Posing as a young boy, she got a job with a Louisville, Kentucky, merchant who hated all things "Yankee." While in his employ, she identified three Rebel spies, two of whom were eventually captured.

Malaria ended her military career. Knowing that she could not seek treatment at an army hospital without having her true sex disclosed, she entered a civilian hospital in Cairo, Illinois, as a woman. Shortly afterward, much to her regret, Emma learned that Franklin Thompson had been officially declared a deserter, an offence punishable by death.

She wrote a book about her experiences called *Unsexed: or the Female Soldier*, which was published by the Bible-sales company she had worked for. In later editions, to suit the temper of Victorian times, the title was changed to *Nurse and Spy*. The book became a bestseller, and she donated all of her royalties to the Sanitary and Christian Commissions, an organization that preceded the Red Cross in caring for wounded veterans.

She married a New Brunswick carpenter, Linus Seelye, in 1867. They settled in the American midwest, where the newly incarnated "Sarah Seelye" gave birth to three children, all of whom died in infancy. Later the couple adopted two sons.

In the 1880s, she determined that she would have to come clean about her status with the Army in order to receive the pension that was her due. Her old comrades in the Second Michigan Regiment helped to have an Act of Congress passed granting her an honourable discharge and the rights that went with it. In 1889, Sarah Emma Edmonds Seelye became the first — and only — woman to be granted membership in the Civil War Veterans' Association.

Representatives of the Grand Army of the Republic conducted her funeral in 1898 and she was buried in the veterans' section of a cemetery in Houston, Texas. Even in death, she adopted a disguise. At her request, her headstone was inscribed simply, "Emma E. Seelye, Army Nurse."

THE RIGHT TO BE BEAUTIFUL

ELIZABETH ARDEN CHANGES THE FACE OF WOMEN

Township of Vaughan, Ontario, 1882 — As a child growing up on the outskirts of Woodbridge, Ontario, Florence Nightingale Graham set a challenging career goal. "I want to be the richest woman in the world," she told anyone who would listen. Although others may have surpassed her wealth through inheritance or royal status, when she died she left an estate worth tens of millions and an imprint on the face of women. Little Flo grew up to be Elizabeth Arden, the queen of a cosmetics empire and one of the most astute retailing entrepreneurs of the twentieth century.

She was one of five children born to Susan and William Graham. In England, her Scottish father made his living racing horses, an enterprise that was frowned upon by his future wife's upper-class family. The pair eloped and came to Canada, where their first child was born in 1871. William became a vegetable peddler, although he still dabbled in horses. Florence, his second youngest daughter, was his best stable helpmate.

It was through her ability at nursing sick horses that Florence determined to follow the path of her famous English nurse namesake. But the rigours of the profession were not for her. "I found I didn't really like looking at sick people. I want to keep people well, and young and beautiful," she explained when she dropped out of school.

According to a biography by Alfred A. Lewis and Constance Woodworth, *Miss Elizabeth Arden: An Unretouched Life*, a chance encounter with a hospital biochemist who was working on a skin cream remedy for acne led her to begin experimenting with beautifying potions of her own in the Graham family kitchen. Strange odours were soon emanating from the wood stove and into the community, causing a local clergyman to fear that the poor family was reduced to cooking rotten eggs. After a hamper of fresh eggs and provisions was dropped at the doorstep, father Graham advised his daughter to get a real job.

Approaching thirty and bored with office work, Graham decided to follow in her brother's footsteps and move to New York City. She started out as a bookkeeper for the Squibb Pharmaceutical Company, but the research laboratories held more fascination for her than numbers. Then, as a beauty parlour trainee, she learned a trendy therapy called "facials," which involved strapping the customer's multiple chins tightly and massaging the skin with glycerin water. She knew there had to be something better.

In 1910, Graham found a kindred spirit in Elizabeth Hubbard, who had developed skin creams, tonics and oil that had marketing potential. Together, they planned to open an upscale "salon" on Fifth Avenue where fashionable women would be pampered and artfully packaged beauty products would be for sale. The partnership fell apart while the gold lettering on Elizabeth Hubbard's name was still drying over the salon's door, but Graham determined to continue alone. Instead of removing the sign she decided to work with it. "Elizabeth" pleased her, but she felt her own last name was too drab for the world of beauty. Reflecting on her favourite poem, Alfred Lord Tennyson's *Enoch Arden*, she settled on "Elizabeth Arden," adding "Mrs." for respectability.

As Elizabeth Arden she prospered. Wealthy socialite clients dubbed her the "little Canadian woman with the magic hands." Through skillful marketing of skin cream products and absolute control of her business, she soon became what she beheld — a wealthy woman who could hold her own in society.

In 1915, she married Thomas Jenkins Lewis, who shared her flair for advertising and marketing. When the marriage ended nineteen years later, Lewis betrayed her trust by promoting the products of archrival Helena Rubenstein. "There is only one Mademoiselle in that world, and that is I," legendary fashion designer Coco Chanel once said. "One Madame, and that is Rubenstein, and one Miss, and that is Arden."

Another marriage, to Russian-born Prince Michael Evlanoff, also ended in divorce in 1942. But whether she was the consort of pseudo-royalty, or married to a pitch man, a Miss or a Mrs., Arden or Graham, the business continued to flourish. By 1944, the U.S. Federal Trade Commission reported that Arden was marketing approximately one thousand different products, and salons featuring her famous red doors were strategically located all over America and in Europe.

The love of horses that her father had fostered also endured. In the early 1930s, Arden-Graham bought a farm in Maine and began raising thoroughbreds. Racing her horses under the name Mrs. Elizabeth Graham, she had an impressive record, which culminated in the 1947 Kentucky Derby win of her stallion, Jet Pilot. Even in her stables she maintained complete autonomy, although her stablehands jokingly called her "Mrs. Mud Pack." Jockeys were instructed to spare the whip on her "darlings."

Wealth allowed her to move in international circles. She had homes all over the world including a castle in Ireland and a ten-room apartment in New York entirely decorated in pink. At five-foot-two, perennially fit, impeccably coiffed and attired, Arden-Graham never looked her age. For many years the slogan of her company was, "Every woman has the right to be beautiful," and Arden did everything she could to claim that right. She is alleged to have gone as far as having her passport photograph retouched.

Fortune magazine once suggested that Arden-Graham "earned more money than any other businesswoman in the history of the United States." She also donated a considerable amount to charity. In 1954, she was honoured by the Canadian Women's Press Club of Toronto. That year, the *Woodbridge News* noted that "Miss Elizabeth Arden" (who was also referred to as "Mrs. Elizabeth Nightingale Graham") attended the opening ceremonies of Dalziel Pioneer Park in Ontario's Humber Valley and planted a tree in the land that had once been her playground.

When she died of a heart attack in 1965, Arden-Graham's age was a mystery. A corporate spokesperson suggested she was eighty-one, born December 31, 1884. However, early Canada Census records indicate that she was probably born in 1882.

Her fortune was estimated at between $30 million and $40 million. Disposing of the business empire proved a complex affair, but Arden-Graham had ensured that her family and faithful employees received substantial bequests. Likewise, her darlings were not forgotten. She insisted that the race horses in training be sold first and that "mares should be sold last, and those with foals should be sold together with their foals." It was hardly a businesslike gesture, but quite beautiful, indeed.

FOR HOME AND COUNTRY

ADELAIDE HOODLESS — WOMAN OF VISION

Stoney Creek, Ontario, 1897 — The turn of the century was a time for maxims, and one that became known throughout the nation was, "You purify society when you purify the home." The maxim-user was a woman with a broad brow, a lush wave of curls and a mission.

Adelaide Hunter was the youngest of twelve children who were raised near Brantford, Ontario, in a clapboard house called "The Willows." Her father, a refugee of the Irish potato famine, died when she was an infant, leaving her mother to struggle to maintain the family farm while instilling in her children a sense of well-being and self-reliance.

Adelaide was twenty-four when she married Hamilton furniture maker John Hoodless and settled into a comfortable middle-class life, which eventually included four children. All may have seemed right with the world to the handsome and poised young mother before tragedy struck in 1889. Her youngest child, John Harold, died of the mysterious ailment known as "summer complaint." In those days, graveyards were filled with tiny headstones. Statistically, one out of every five Canadian children died, and Adelaide set out to discover the root cause of such heavy casualties.

When she learned that her child's death may have been caused by something as innocuous as milk, she began a crusade that would last her lifetime. Without benefit of refrigeration, farmers delivered their milk in open cans to populated areas. Flies that swarmed in summer streets found their way into kitchens where ice boxes were inefficient and rare. Hoodless was convinced that the high infant mortality rate had more to do with ignorance of good nutrition and sanitation than it did with "God's will."

Within months, the grieving mother appeared before the fledgling Young Women's Christian Association in Hamilton with a proposal to include cooking and domestic science in their courses. Soon the local school board was sending pupils to the YWCA and teachers were being provided with instruction.

In 1893, YWCA delegate Hoodless attended the Columbian Exposition in Chicago where issues such as suffrage and women's working conditions were hot topics. She met a kindred spirit in Lady Aberdeen, the wife of Canada's new Governor-General, and a tireless organizer of causes relating to women. Consequently, Hoodless set wheels into motion that helped create the YWCA as a national organization. Lady Aberdeen called on her in Hamilton after the Chicago experience and the result was the formation of the National Council of Women, which held its first annual meeting in April, 1894.

Over the following two years, Hoodless gave more than sixty speeches about the importance of domestic science.

Through her platform she was able to encourage the development of courses in schools across the country. She wrote a guidebook on nutrition that became a nationwide fixture in the kitchen. It was apparent that her goals were far larger than any food fad, and she was able to enlist support and donations for the establishment of an Institute of Household Science at the Ontario College of Agriculture in Guelph.

In February 1897, 101 women and one man (farmer Erland Lee) attended a meeting at Stoney Creek, Ontario, where the formation of a sister organization to the national federated Farmers' Institute was discussed. Under Hoodless's guiding hand and with the banner slogan "for home and country," Women's Institutes soon formed all over the country. Members were committed to the notion that "a nation cannot rise above the level of its homes." The Institute became an international organization that expanded to include country women in more than one hundred nations.

Hoodless had a definite knack for getting things started. With Lady Aberdeen she helped form the Victorian Order of Nurses to provide care in frontier communities. She excelled at fund raising and her poised presentations made her a popular speaker.

In the middle of a speech to a Toronto audience of the Federation of Women's Clubs in 1910, fifty-two-year-old Adelaide Hoodless, who had been bothered by a headache all day, smiled, took a sip of water and fell lifeless to the floor. At the time, she was just beginning to investigate the possibility of establishing technical and trade schools for young women, which explains why she is universally acknowledged as Canada's "Woman of Vision."

OUR LADY OF THE SOURDOUGH

MARTHA BLACK'S "BELOVED YUKON" ADVENTURE

Dawson City, Yukon Territory, 1898 — When Chicago socialite Martha Louise Munger Purdy set out over the Chilkoot Pass in 1898 with thousands of other Klondike dreamers, she was looking for adventure and whatever came her way. In the thrall of gold fever, the refined thirty-two-year-old had arranged for her two sons to stay with her parents in Chicago. At the last minute, her wealthy businessman husband, William Purdy, decided to head for the Sandwich Islands instead. Their failing marriage ended when Martha boarded the steamer *Utopia* bound for Skagway. Martha Louise had embarked on a life-transforming journey far from the froth and frivolity of America's Gay Nineties that would eventually see her become the First Lady of the Yukon and the second woman to sit in the Canadian Parliament.

When her party cleared the North-West Mounted Police

checkpoint at Lake Tagish, it was logged as the 14,405th to enter the rapids that led to wild and woolly Dawson City. Her money and her mettle had helped her to get that far, driven by a rumour of a million dollars in gold dust, a legacy she would share if she could find it and lay the claim.

When this failed to happen, however, Martha staked a few claims and settled into a log cabin across the Klondike River in a district known as "Lousetown," famous for its brothels. To complicate matters, she soom discovered that she was pregnant. Considering the scarcity of food and medical assistance, the odds were stacked against her survival, but on January 31, 1899, she gave birth to a healthy son named Lyman.

Neighbours rallied to supply food, fuel and bedding, and grit-eyed miners crowded the cabin to marvel at the simple beauty of a baby. "We became self-reliant," Martha noted years later. "We knew what it was to get along without the amenities of so-called civilized life."

The winter saw a typhoid epidemic and a fire all but consume Dawson City. By spring, those "cheechakoos" (tenderfoots) who had survived were elevated to the more respectful status of "sourdoughs," in honour of the yeastless bread that was their dietary staple.

That summer Martha returned to her father's home after a landslide came within thirty metres of sweeping her cabin into the river. She found life in Chicago stifling. In 1901, with some profits from her claims and the support of her family, she returned to her "beloved Yukon" and started a sawmill business.

At thirty-eight, the now divorced mother of three married a Dawson lawyer who was seven years her junior. George Black had spent a couple of years mining before returning to his law practice and the pursuit of Conservative political ambitions. In 1912, he was appointed Commissioner of the Yukon and, for the next four years Martha Black served as chatelaine of Government House. At her first reception she served one thousand sandwiches and forty cakes, accompanied by massive quantities of salads and plenty of ice cream. Although her staff was astounded, the new First Lady understood the appetite of the hardy souls of the Yukon.

George Black resigned as Commissioner in 1916 and began recruiting the Yukon Infantry Company, in which he was a captain. Martha bucked bureaucracy to travel with the men when they left to serve in Europe during the First World War. While George and company fought in France, Martha crusaded for the Yukon in London, giving lectures and assisting volunteers. Her knowledge of Yukon flora earned her a fellowship in the Royal Geographical Society. Lyman, the son she bore in Dawson, was invested with the Military Cross by King George V.

When the war ended, George Black resumed his political career, representing his Yukon constituency from 1921 until 1935, when he was sidelined by illness. Friends pressured Martha to run in his place, and the seventy-year-old sourdough rose to the challenge, campaigning vigorously throughout the territory to win by 134 votes, although the majority of other Conservative candidates suffered a rousing defeat by William Lyon Mackenzie King's Liberals.

For the next five years, Martha Black and parliamentary pioneer Agnes Macphail were the only females in the House of Commons. When George regained his health, he also regained his seat, which Martha insisted she had merely been "keeping warm."

The transformation of the Chicago socialite was complete by 1949, when she received the Order of the British Empire for her contribution to Yukon life.

"For There Shall Be
A Performance"

Sister Aimee Semple McPherson Finds Her Voice

Mount Forest, Ontario, 1915 — When evangelist Jean Sharpe learned that Aimee Semple McPherson was coming to her Victory Mission in the rural, southwestern Ontario town of Mount Forest, she was inspired by the writings of the apostle Luke. "Blessed is she that believeth, for there shall be a performance of those things that were told her from the Lord." However, McPherson's first "performance" was somewhat of a disappointment, since it attracted a paltry audience of two men and a boy. Four sermons later, the attendance was no better and Sister Aimee was getting antsy.

"I surveyed the scene and sought to lay my plans for a siege of souls," McPherson wrote in her memoir, *This and That*. With that, the slender brunette hit upon an idea that was to prove her trademark for the next quarter-century — she pulled a stunt.

Garbed in white, McPherson hauled a chair to the middle of town. As the sun set, she stood on the chair with her eyes closed and her arms raised to the heavens. A crowd of curious onlookers gathered and when McPherson felt the time was ripe she jumped off the chair and shouted, "People follow me!" Then she ran down the street to the meeting hall, hustled her followers inside, locked the door and commenced preaching. The captive audience was soon captivated.

"If you are annoyed over attendance, why not try the chair-and-prayer method at some busy intersection? I can heartily recommend it and practically guarantee that it will work," McPherson later advised wannabe sermonizers. Her stunts, combined with her charisma, created an indomitable force in evangelism that would lead her to become the most famous and infamous preacher of the Roaring Twenties and the Dirty Thirties.

Sister Aimee grew up near Ingersoll, Ontario, the daughter of a Methodist father and a Salvation Army mother. At seventeen, she married Robert Semple, a Pentecostal preacher and blacksmith. In 1912, they travelled to China where Robert planned to become a missionary, but he died of malaria soon after their arrival, leaving his pregnant widow to fend for herself. Returning to the continent with her newborn daughter, Aimee married a grocery clerk, Harold McPherson. Following the birth of their son, Aimee began her itinerant preaching and Harold divorced her on the grounds of desertion.

There was no particular organization to accompany the professional preacher. Fire and brimstone gypsies travelled what became known as "the Sawdust Trail" after the ground cover that they spread over the dirt floors beneath their tents. With her mother, Minnie Kennedy, serving as her business manager, McPherson barnstormed across the continent, starting on the Atlantic coast and ending up in California in 1918.

From dingy halls, she soon graduated to huge auditoriums and tours that took her to Europe and Australia. By 1923, her coffers had swelled enough to allow the construction of a $1.25 million, 5,000-seat church in Los Angeles. The Angelus Temple became the home of the Church of the Foursquare Gospel, complete with its own radio station and Bible school. "I don't like the tinkle of silver, but the rustle of paper," McPherson announced when the collection plates circulated.

Whether embroiled in law suits or organizing soup kitchens, Sister Aimee made the most of every publicity opportunity. Her most famous "stunt" occurred when she vanished from a California beach on May 26, 1926. Thousands showed up to comb the sand, along with boats and search planes. When she finally surfaced a month later in Mexico with a bizarre tale of kidnapping and torture, it raised more than eyebrows. A grand jury hearing convened to look into allegations that included perjury and conspiracy to perpetrate a hoax. Ultimately, no charges were laid, but the front page coverage — and the speculation that McPherson's disappearance was related to her involvement with the temple's married radio operator — filled her pews more than ever.

McPherson's personal life was as fraught with breakdowns as her public persona. A rift with her mother ended in a $100,000 settlement after Aimee reportedly broke Minnie's nose in a slugfest. In 1936, she accused her daughter and other church associates of conspiring to wrest control from her. McPherson lost the bitter court battle that ensued. Her third marriage was also doomed to failure. None of that stopped her from preaching and building more churches.

Sister Aimee was in Oakland, California, on September 26, 1944. She led a parade, preached to a packed house and planned to dedicate a church the following day. Her Sunday sermon, "Going My Way," had already been announced, but the next morning she was found dead in her hotel room at the age of fifty-three. Although initially reported as a heart attack, the cause of death was later revealed as the apparent consequence of an accidental overdose of barbiturates.

Sister Aimee Semple McPherson's performance had ended.

PART FOUR
SPORTS

THE TURN-OF-THE-CENTURY TERMINATOR

SINGING ON THE GREENS

THE RUNNING MAN

JUST FOR THE FUN OF IT

TURN HIM LOOSE!

THE BIG TRAIN THAT COULD

GILDING THE SASKATOON LILY

THE TURN-OF-THE-CENTURY TERMINATOR

LOUIS CYR AND EIGHTEEN FAT MEN

Montreal, Quebec, 1892 — Nothing could have prepared the thugs who roamed the toughest district of Montreal for the newest police recruit. Louis Cyr was a massive man and a virtual block of muscle. At his peak, the fair-haired strongman had a 152-centimetre (60-inch) chest, 84-centimetre (33-inch) thighs and biceps that were the size of a fit woman's waist. When he confronted the underworld ruffians of Sainte-Cunégonde, he had no weapon other than brute strength. "At first the arrested ones endeavoured to put up a fight," reported the Montreal *Star*. "Cyr, taking one under each arm and carrying the other in a vice-like grip in front of him, marched off to the station with all three prisoners off the ground." But lifting three men was a fractional display of Cyr's strength. In 1895, he backlifted a platform holding eighteen fat men weighing 1,967 kilograms (4,337 pounds).

From birth, the Canadian Hercules seemed destined for big things. When he entered the world on October 10, 1863 at St-Cyprien-de-Napierville, south of Montreal, the eldest of the seventeen Cyr children weighed an astounding 8.2 kilograms (18 pounds). His father was a farmer of unremarkable stature, but his mother was statuesque. She could hoist two full grain sacks at a time. This was a feat that her fair-haired son (baptised Noe Cyprien) matched at twelve years old, when he abandoned all formal schooling to take his first job working in a woodlot.

The family moved to Lowell, Massachusetts when Noe was fifteen. Lowell was a textile centre and the bustling town attracted so many French-Canadian workers that it became known as "Little Canada." In preparation for the trip, young Cyr learned English. His mother decided that he should have a name more in keeping with the Anglo-Saxon tongue and selected "Louis" in honour of the French kings. She also took it upon herself to apply curling irons to his long blonde hair. Although his age would normally have precluded him from heavy work, Louis Cyr impressed the first foreman he met by hoisting a 170-kilogram (350-pound) roll of cloth. At the age of eighteen, he won his first strongman contest. He lifted a Percheron horse on his back and was promptly declared the strongest man in Massachusetts.

At the celebration in honour of this triumph, Louis met Melina Comtois, a wisp of a woman who took over the curling iron chores after she became his wife in 1882. Melina had also been targeted for courtship by another French-Canadian, David Michaud, Canada's reigning undefeated strongman for a decade. When Michaud challenged Cyr to a title match in Quebec City, it was said to be as much a challenge of romantic revenge as it was a desire to maintain control of his title.

The champion chose boulders as the challenge. They were marked with weights from 45 to 227 kilograms (100 to 500 pounds), with one huge rock identified only by a question mark. Rain created a muddy playing field for the two giants, but both were able to raise the second-largest rock. The showdown came over the rock of questionable weight. When it was over, Cyr was victorious and the answer to the question of the rock's weight was 237 kilograms (522 pounds).

Louis Cyr was formally designated the "strongest man in the world" in 1896 when he confronted Swedish champion August Johnson in a competition that lasted more than three hours. "I can defeat any man in the world; but no man can defeat this elephant," Johnson is reported to have commented.

For all his strength, Cyr also had weaknesses — the greatest being gluttony. From childhood, he associated food with physical power and his heroic eating habits became part of his legend. During a twenty-three-month tour of England, the gentry were almost as impressed by his 9-kilograms (20-pounds) a day meat capacity as they were with his ability to lift 250 kilograms (551 pounds) with the middle finger of one hand. Ultimately, diet proved the erstwhile Samson's downfall. By the age of thirty-seven, he suffered from Bright's disease and subsisted on a diet of milk.

In 1906, Cyr participated in his final championship. The debilitated, forty-four-year-old met the challenge of superbly conditioned, twenty-nine-year-old Hector Decarie. Surprisingly, the two gladiators ended in a tie, after Cyr hoisted a 1,302-kilogram (2,8700-pound) platform that Decarie could not budge. Then in a measure of grace, Cyr retired forever. One month after his forty-ninth birthday, he died.

"He used power...nothing but power," wrote Ben

Weider, the founder of the International Federation of Body-builders, who spent his own Quebec childhood imitating the feats of the legendary Louis Cyr. "What a modern coach could do with a man of his muscular power heaven only knows."

SINGING ON THE GREENS

GEORGE S. LYON — CANADA'S SWINGINGEST OLYMPIAN

St. Louis, Missouri, 1904 — Golf was played as an Olympic event only once in the history of the Games, and top honours went to a forty-six-year-old Canadian. George Seymour Lyon, a golfer of unconventional swing and attitude, accepted his gold medal and commemorative silver cup after walking through the dining room of the Glen Echo Country Club on his hands.

Lyon did not hold a putter until he was thirty-eight, but by then he was already one of Canada's most accomplished athletes in a variety of other sports, including rugby, baseball, soccer, lawn bowling, curling. At eighteen he set a Canadian record in the pole vault. He represented Canada at cricket eleven times and once scored 238 not out for his club, another Canadian record.

Golf was a game he took up on a dare in 1896. He never looked back. His swing has been described as "a haphazard, if ruthless, swipe at the ball," and his stance owed more to cricket than golf. Lyon played the game aggressively rather than pensively, and he took great delight in walloping the ball. Beneath his unconventional form was a truly competitive temperament. After only one season of play, he made the semifinals of the Canadian amateur championship, a title which he eventually won eight times.

The Third Modern Olympiad in 1904 was held in St. Louis, but the Games themselves were almost totally overwhelmed by other events, including the Russo-Japanese War and the St. Louis World's Fair. There were no opening or closing ceremonies; many European nations did not even bother to send a team.

In the golf competition, Toronto's George Lyon placed in the top half of the thirty-six-hole qualifying round that reduced the field of mainly American golfers from seventy-five to thirty-two. It was during this time that reporters twigged to Lyon's "coal-heaver's swing," as well as his penchant for singing on the greens when the round was over and for telling jokes to his competitors.

In his semifinal round against U.S. Pacific Coast champion Francis Newton, Lyon's pin-high drive was recorded at an amazing 273.4 metres (299 yards). When the personality-packed Canadian triumphed over twenty-three-year-old American amateur champion Chandler Egan to win the event, the St. Louis *Globe Democrat* cited his "iron nerves" and "prepondering wisdom, born of longer experience."

Lyon could have had two Olympic victories to his credit. In 1908, he was scheduled to play in the London Olympics; however, an internal dispute among British golfers led them to boycott the games. Lyon was the only other entrant, but he refused to receive a gold medal by default. Golf has never since been entertained as an Olympic event.

As the veteran captain of his home course, the Lambton Golf and Country Club in Toronto, Lyon continued to play golf and encourage newcomers to the sport. In 1924, his son, Fred, took the Ontario Junior Championship. Lyon himself went on to win the Canadian Senior Championship ten times, placing second on four other occasions.

Until the age of seventy-eight, George S. Lyon, Canada's only golfing Olympian, shot his age for eighteen holes. He died the following year in 1938. To this day, the members of the Lambton Golf and Country Club open and close their season with the song that George S. would sing with gusto at the slightest provocation, "My Wild Irish Rose."

THE RUNNING MAN

TOM "WILDFIRE" LONGBOAT GIVES HIS EVERYTHING

Boston, Massachusetts, 1907 — Greed and racial innuendo peppered the career of Canada's first national sports hero of the twentieth century. In other circumstances, marathon runner Tom Longboat might have become a wealthy and venerated athlete. Instead he ended up working as a garbage-man. "Maybe all I'm good for now is sweeping leaves, but if I can help the kids and show them how to be good runners and how to live a clean life, I'm satisfied," Longboat told the Toronto *Globe* thirty years after running the Boston Marathon in record time.

Tom Longboat's Onandaga name was Cogwagee, meaning "Everything." He was born in a log house on the Six Nations Reserve near Brantford, Ontario in 1887. His father died when Tom was five, and much of his childhood was spent helping his mother on their small farm. He resented the English-language education provided by the Anglican mission boarding school that drew him away from his own culture and the aid of his family. At twelve, his formal education ended and he became a transient farm labourer.

Mohawk runner, Bill Davis, took Longboat under his wing after watching him finish second at the Caledon Fair in 1905. Longboat began training every day, extending his distances gradually. The following Victoria Day, he won the Caledon 8-kilometre (5-mile) race by more than 400 metres.

The booming steeltown of Hamilton held a prestigious 30.5-kilometre (19-mile) foot race around Burlington Bay every year. In 1906, the crowd chuckled as a tall, native competitor took his place at the starting line wearing cheap canvas running shoes, threadbare cotton bathing trunks and a baggy sweatshirt. Although he ran awkwardly, with his feet kicking sideways and his hands held hip high, the onlookers' laughter turned to cheers when Longboat beat the field by a full three minutes. Two more victories that year confirmed his abilities.

On a cold April morning in 1907, Tom Longboat became a national hero when he sailed past more than one hundred competitors to win the Boston Marathon. He was showered and eating steak before the other runners finished.

Longboat's winning streak continued, but coping with fame and the wiles of the world was not his forte. The YMCA suspended him for a curfew violation, and for breaking smoking and drinking restrictions. Two Irishmen, Tom Flanagan and Jim O'Rourke, took an interest in him and Longboat began running for the Irish-Canadian Athletic Club, all the while dodging suspicions that his caretakers were placing bets on the side. The U.S. Amateur Athletic Union declared him a professional. Flanagan gave Longboat a job in a cigar shop to show Canadian authorities that the runner had independent means.

Despite a case of boils that caused him to miss the Olympic trials, Longboat was named to the 1908 Canadian team. He was among the leaders in the marathon when he collapsed in the final quarter of the race. Rumours flew that he had been overtrained, undertrained or drugged by gambling interests. A disappointed Longboat suggested that he had run his last race.

Not surprisingly, Flanagan persuaded him otherwise. Soon afterward he was winning races throughout Ontario and setting new records, prompting Canadian Athletic Union president William Stark to declare him "the greatest long distance runner of the century."

Tom Longboat turned professional on December 15, 1908 when he raced Olympic gold medalist Dorando Pietri at Madison Square Garden. He won $3,000 when the Italian collapsed six laps from the finish. Again, Longboat was claimed as a Canadian hero. He and his Mohawk bride, Lauretta Maracle, were given a wedding reception at Toronto's Massey Hall.

One of the biggest match races in history took place on February 5, 1909, when the Canadian dubbed "Wildfire" met international champion Alfie Shrubb in the run for the professional championship of the world. Shrubb conceded after 39 kilometres (24 miles) and Longboat jogged to a standing ovation.

Meanwhile, Flanagan cashed-out, selling his contract to an American promoter for $2,000. Longboat lost his next race, and his contract was sold again, this time for $700. No longer invincible, he was tarred by the press as "lazy," and a suspended sentence for drunkenness in 1911 tarnished his image.

Interest in marathon running paled with the outbreak of the First World War in 1914. Longboat was one of 292

Six Nations warriors to go to the front. In France, he ran dispatches through the trenches. Twice wounded, he was once declared dead during a debacle in Belgium. When he returned home, he discovered that his wife had taken the news seriously enough to remarry. He started a new family and took whatever work he could find. When he died of pneumonia at the age of sixty-one, the funeral service was conducted in Onondaga, a language Tom Longboat never forgot.

Just For The Fun Of It

Tommy Ryan Turns Ten-Pins into Five

Toronto, 1909 — Imagine how it must feel to forget to patent a million-dollar invention — a game that has become Canada's largest participant sport, enjoyed by millions and profitable to many. "I was hustling so much... well, I forgot," admitted Tommy Ryan, an elfin, jovial entrepreneur, who favoured wearing a bow-tie that squirted water.

The game Ryan created was five-pin bowling, a compaction of the ten-pin game. Bowling artifacts have been unearthed in Egyptian tombs. An outdoor version of the game played on grass with wooden pegs became such a popular diversion from field work that King Henry III of England passed a law forbidding it. Variations of the game have been played by Celtic Helvitii and by ancient Polynesian cultures. Ryan's refinements, however, were uniquely Canadian.

The Canadian 5-Pin Bowlers' Association dates the

invention of this game as November, 1909, although Ryan could never be pinned to an exact date. He was promoting boxing matches, dabbling in horse racing and running his own ten-pin bowling alley when he devised the game. "I was the biggest sucker in the world," Ryan said on reflection. He was also one of the game's greatest boosters for more than half a century.

Thomas Francis Ryan was born in Guelph, Ontario in 1872. From an early age, he was good at games that involved throwing spheres. While he was working as an invoice clerk in Toronto, his after-hours skill as a baseball pitcher attracted an offer from the Baltimore Orioles. Instead, Ryan opened a billiards academy that catered to his many friends in the sporting fraternity. In 1905, he diversified, installing the first ten-pin bowling lanes in Canada above a jewellery store not far from the business district.

Ryan intended to attract a toney crowd. At a time when bowling alleys were considered something akin to the devil's work, he offered an emporium featuring potted tropical plants, a string orchestra and private memberships. The ten polished wood alleys designed by Chicago experts at a cost of $45,000, however, failed to earn their keep.

Although his carriage trade patrons included the likes of retail magnate Sir John Eaton and the elite legal minds of Osgoode Hall, the rigours of the game proved too taxing. "The ten-pin ball was too heavy for the type of person I had induced to bowl," Ryan told sportswriter Al Nickleson. "Some hadn't used their muscles in years. They'd bowl one or two games, then play bridge in my office while I supplied adhesive tape for their thumbs."

Ryan's solution was obvious. Instead of a 7.2-kilogram (16-pound) behemoth of a ball, he opted for a palm-held, light-weight ball without any troublesome digit-holes. He even supplied the balls, eliminating cartage problems for his white-collar customers.

Smaller balls meant smaller pins. Ryan's father, a practical mechanic, whittled down five ten-pins with a lathe. Then Ryan figured out a new scoring system for a game that asks its players to knock down five pins configured in a 91-centimetre (36-inch) triangle by rolling a ball down a narrow 18.3-metre (60-foot) solid surface. Each bowler was allowed ten "frames" per game and a maximum of three balls per frame. A score could only be counted if the bowler knocked over the Number Four corner pin, a stipulation that Ryan found resulted in no uncertain "blasphemy."

Noise and damage control characterized the first few riotous years of five-pin bowling. The lighter pins fairly flew through the air, sending the setters (young men known as pin-boys) scurrying for cover. By 1912, numerous complaints had arisen over errant pins crashing through windows and endangering passers-by on the street below. Ryan responded with innovation, adding a rubber collar to the belly of each pin. This served as a shock absorber and lowered the decibel level. Players also saw their scores soar, since the added girth of the collar allowed the ball to connect with greater frequency. In 1921, Bill Bromfield knocked off the first perfect game, scoring 450 points. The sport thrived and "trundlers" were soon flocking to bowling centres across the country.

In later years, Tommy Ryan found other diversions to capture his imagination, including judging beauty pageants and conducting antique auctions from his sprawling three-storey mansion, once the home of farm implement mogul, Hart Massey. At the age of seventy-eight, he spearheaded the drive that ended an eighty-five-year ban on Sunday sports in Toronto. A decade later, in 1960, he was honoured at Canada's first Civic Bowling Week celebrations. When he died the following year, he did not regret the lost profits he might have taken from the game. In the words of Tommy Ryan, "I don't care, as long as people are having fun."

Turn Him Loose!

Tom Three Persons Tames Cyclone

Calgary, 1912 — There is an old prairie adage that suggests, "There never was a horse that can't be rode, or ever a cowboy that can't be thrown." Ultimately, that is the spirit of rodeo — a contest between human and animal, which combines sport and entertainment with commerce and romanticism for the Old West. There have been many confrontations between those with two legs and those with four, but when Tom Three Persons met a black bronco named Cyclone, the ride went down in history.

Three Persons, a Blood Indian from Cardston, Alberta, was the only Canadian to make it to the finals of the saddle bronc riding competition at the first Calgary Stampede in 1912. Under the guiding hand of vaudeville rodeo maestro Guy Weadick of Wyoming, hundreds of cowboys showed up to vie for prize money put up by Alberta's Big Four — Pat Burns, A.E. Cross, George Burns and A.J. Maclean

— but the majority were experienced American cowboys and hard-riding Mexican vaqueros. To make matters worse, Three Persons drew Cyclone, a horse that had thrown 127 cowboys in seven years of bucking. There was no eight- or ten-second time limit in those days; the ride simply ended when the horse stopped bucking or the rider stopped riding. Cyclone had never stopped.

Three Persons was the last competitor in the event and thousands crowded the stands to watch. The infield betting held that the brawny twenty-four-year-old would not last four jumps. With his gravity-defying leaps, Cyclone had already beaten one of the best cowboys in the country, Pirmez Creek's Clem Gardner. When Three Persons shouted "turn him loose" there was no turning back.

"Bucking, twisting, swapping ends and resorting to every artifice of the outlaw, Cyclone swept across the field," reported the *Calgary Herald*. "The Indian was jarred from one side of the saddle to the other, but as the crowds cheered themselves hoarse he settled every time into the saddle and waited for the next lurch or twist."

When bucking did not work, Cyclone turned to his trademark vertical rearing tactics, but Three Persons was ready for the acrobatics. He let out a bellow that brought Cyclone down to earth. Soon the pair were galloping across the field like old friends in a hurry.

Spectators cheered wildly and hundreds of native people galloped their own horses up and down the field in celebration. When he was inducted into the Canadian Rodeo Historical Association's Hall of Fame in 1983 it was acknowledged that "Tom Three Persons became a hero that day."

For years afterward, Three Persons returned to the Calgary Stampede, but he never won another world title. He became a successful rancher, raising purebred Hereford cattle and thoroughbred horses. At sixty, he suffered a broken pelvic bone while trying to stop a young horse from breaking a corral, and he died three years later in 1949. It was the largest funeral ever seen in Cardston. In his obituary, the *Albertan* said that when Tom Three Persons tamed Cyclone he "rode into a niche in the hearts of westerners who will remember him as long as cattle graze in the foothills and cowboys ride after them."

THE BIG TRAIN THAT COULD

ALL-ROUND ALL-STAR LIONEL CONACHER

Toronto, 1922 — Although his formal schooling never went beyond the eighth grade, Lionel Conacher may have owed one of Canada's most illustrious sporting careers to the education system. There were ten children in the Conacher family. Money was tight and the working-class streets of Toronto were rough and tumble. A wise headmaster at Jesse Ketchum Public School, where Lionel was a student, realized that mandating a program of organized sports could help preserve some sense of order. Through sports, young Lionel saw a way out of poverty, and he excelled in every one he tried. When he was named Canada's Male Athlete of the Half-Century in 1950, it was for outstanding achievement in wrestling, boxing, football, lacrosse, hockey, rugby and baseball.

Conacher played football in the Toronto Rugby League when he was twelve. At sixteen he won the Ontario 125-pound wrestling championship. By 1920, the twenty-year-old

Conacher had boxed himself to the light-heavyweight championship of Canada. The following year, he stood his ground in an exhibition match with world heavyweight champion Jack Dempsey.

Football was his favourite game. He could run the 100 yards in less than ten seconds. When the Toronto Argos defeated the Edmonton Eskimos 23 to 0 in the 1921 Grey Cup, Conacher contributed fifteen points.

No one sport was big enough for Conacher. On one legendary day in 1922 he hit a triple in the final inning of the Ontario baseball championship for the winning Hillcrest team. Still holding the victory wreath, he jumped into a car, changed uniforms and led the Toronto Maitlands to a provincial championship in lacrosse.

Hockey was where the money was, and Conacher turned pro in 1925 as a member of the Pittsburgh Pirates in the expanding National Hockey League. He had only been skating for seven years. "I laced on skates for the first time at the age of sixteen, and you'll never know the humiliation and utter weariness of the long hours which I spent on the rink with younger and much more skilled players before I won a post in junior circles," Conacher admitted. He compensated for his awkwardness on the ice by becoming a great tactician, stopping pucks with his knee and calculating angles with split-second timing. There was always some steam left in the player who was known as "the Big Train." In his 11-year NHL career as a defenceman he scored 80 goals and 105 assists. His name was engraved on the Stanley Cup twice.

By the end of his playing days, Conacher's battle scars chronicled a saga of victory and confrontation. He bore as many as 600 stitches patchworked over his six-foot-one frame, including 150 from the shoulders up. His nose had been rearranged eight times.

In 1937, Conacher moved to the political backbenches as the Liberal MPP for Toronto Bracondale. For twelve years, constituents brought their problems to the office he kept just a block from where he was born. Appropriately, he served as chairman of the Ontario Athletic Commission and devoted himself to championing needs he understood, such as recreational facilities in city parks.

In 1949, the federal Liberals pitted popular hero Lionel Conacher against Communist Party leader Tim Buck for the working-class Toronto Trinity riding. Conacher held that seat until he died.

It was May 24, 1954, and the Members of Parliament were playing their annual softball game with the parliamentary press corps. In the sixth inning, Conacher lifted a flyball for a triple. He was racing to third base when his heart failed. Twenty minutes later, "the Big Train" stopped forever.

Gilding The Saskatoon Lily

Ethel Catherwood Flies Through the Air

Amsterdam Olympics, 1928 — The high jump was the last event in which Canada had an entry in the Ninth Olympiad. As nineteen-year-old Ethel Catherwood attempted to stretch and flex in the chilled Dutch air, the Canadian women's team already led the forty-nation points standing. Cameras poised to capture the moment in which the lanky and lithe Catherwood was suspended over the bar. She was the most photographed athlete at the 1928 Games, and she remains the only Canadian woman to have won an individual gold medal in Olympic track and field competition. The *New York Times* called her "the prettiest of all the girl athletes." Canadians knew her as "the Saskatoon Lily."

Ethel Catherwood was born in Haldimand County, Ontario in 1909, but she was raised in Saskatchewan. Her ability in what was then known as the "running high jump" became evident when she entered the Saskatoon city championships in the summer of 1926 and equalled the Canadian record of 1.511 metres (4 feet, 11½ inches). That Labour Day, the third-year high school student went to Regina and broke the world high jump record. "Her performance overshadowed the championship events for men," noted her hometown newspaper the *Saskatoon Phoenix*. "Even the auto races failed to furnish the thrill that spectators derived when she beat her old record."

Mining millionaire Teddy Oke, a noted patron of amateur sport, quickly transported Ethel and her sister, Ginger, to Toronto. He sent them both to business school and gave them jobs in his brokerage offices, which were largely staffed by female athletes. Catherwood became a member of the Parkdale Ladies Athletic Club and Oke hired veteran coach Walter Knox to hone her technique.

Sportswriters were soon as smitten with the long-legged Western Canadian as Oke. "From the instant this tall, graceful girl from the Prairies tossed aside her long, flowing cloak of purple and made her first leap, the fans fell for her," wrote one. "A flower-like face of rare beauty above a long, slim body clad in pure white ... she looked like a tall, strange lily — and was immediately christened by the crowd 'The Saskatoon Lily.'"

The Lily blossomed at the final Olympic trials held during a heat wave in Halifax in July of 1928. Five thousand spectators showed up to cheer what the *Halifax Chronicle* called "the greatest collection of women athletic stars in Canada." Ethel Catherwood jumped 1.6 metres (5 feet 3 inches), reclaiming the world record from South Africa's Marjorie Clark and setting a mark that stood as the Canadian record until 1954.

The 1928 Olympics were a triumph for Canada's six-member women's team. By the time Catherwood's high jump event took place on the final day, the track team had taken one gold medal, two silver medals and a bronze. All eyes in the stadium focused on the Canadian beauty, who carried a rag doll and a ukulele with her wherever she went.

There were twenty-three contestants in the high jump, including Holland's own Carolina Gisolf who had beaten Catherwood's world record by a fraction of an inch. Wrapped in her red Hudson's Bay blanket, the Canadian contender tried to stay warm between jumps on the uncharacteristically cold August day. Only the competitors were allowed on the field, so Catherwood had to fend for herself until friendly members of the Belgian team took it upon themselves to cloak her after each jump. She only placed seventeenth in the qualifying events, but in the afternoon final her grace and co-ordination proved unstoppable.

The leap that gilded Catherwood was a full half inch less than her personal best, but that final gold medal gave the Canadian women's team an overall victory. "She was lifted to the shoulders of Canadians, athletes and spectators alike, and smilingly received the plaudits of the huge crowd," crowed the Toronto *Evening Telegraph*.

The first Olympic Games in which Canadian women participated was almost their last. Pundits from the Pope to McGill University's Dr. A.S. Lamb argued that strenuous sport was physiologically and psychologically unsuitable for women. The proof of the performance of Catherwood and her teammates resoundingly refuted such theories.

After her hero's homecoming welcome, Catherwood was courted for stardom, but she rejected Hollywood's beckon. In 1929, she and her sister moved to the United States, where Ethel married and settled in San Francisco. Her benefactor, Teddy Oke, was said to be so disheartened by the departure of his dream athlete that he abandoned plans to build a women's sports palace in Toronto.

The once-soaring high jumper never competed again.

PART FIVE

ADVENTURE, DISCOVERY AND ART

FOOLS RUSH IN

A HATFUL OF GRAIN

THE GREAT CANADIAN KISSER

ONE WITH THE SOIL

THE PIE MAN

BORN OF FIRE AND BLOOD

SHE DID IT HER WAY

THE WONDER MUSH REVOLUTION

FOOLS RUSH IN

MARTIN FROBISHER LEADS THE FIRST GOLD RUSH

Kodlunarn Island, Northwest Territories, 1578 — Klondike poet Robert Service said it best when he wrote: "Strange things are done in the midnight sun by the men who moil for gold." In three remarkable voyages to the Canadian Arctic, adventurer and master mariner Martin Frobisher proved this to be true. His quest for gold cost forty lives, and the ton of ore that his crew excavated by hand turned out to be worthless "fool's gold." Even his search for a northwest passage proved to be folly — the "strait" he thought was a transcontinental channel turned out to be the bay that now bears his name.

As a teenager, Frobisher left his native England to crew aboard various Elizabethan expeditions. Like many of the daredevil marine careerists of the day, he dabbled in piracy. Early on, it became apparent that Queen Elizabeth I had a soft spot for Frobisher and his impetuous plundering of

Spanish ships, especially since a share of his booty went to Her Majesty's coffers. When Frobisher decided that he wanted to find the legendary northwest passage to Cathay, he took his plan to the Queen's court. "It is still the only thing left undone, whereby a notable mind might be made famous and remarkable," he noted.

Although the privately owned Muscovy Company held the licence for such exploration, the Privy Council prevailed to give Frobisher a crack at it. Michael Lok, a Muscovy director, became Frobisher's champion. He corralled eighteen investors and personally contributed £700 to finance shipbuilding and outfitting.

On June 7, 1576, the Queen waved a farewell. Foul weather drove them to the shores of Greenland, where four men were lost in a pinnace accompanying the two main ships, the *Gabriell* and *Michaell*. Captain Owen Griffyn of the *Michaell* decided to turn back. Arriving in London, he reported the rest lost.

But Frobisher continued, noting that "the sea must needs have an ending." Finally, he found a "great gutte, bay or passage" which he thought was the route to Asia.

Five of Frobisher's seamen disappeared after going to shore with a native. No trace of them was ever found; however, native folk lore indicates that "they died in our land ... we did not harm them." In an apparent attempt to counter his loss, Frobisher lured an Inuit aboard, whereupon the terrified man bit off his own tongue.

The return to England that October was cause for celebration. Frobisher handed Michael Lok a chunk of glistening black rock which he said was the "first thing that he found in the new land." Three assayers identified the rock as marcasite, a crystallized version of iron pyrite commonly known as "fool's gold." However, a fourth, an Italian named Agnello, announced that he found gold in the samples. Whether the sample had been doctored or whether gold actually existed remains a subject of debate. "It is necessary to know how to flatter nature," explained the enigmatic Agnello.

Within months, a second expedition was fully funded. Queen Elizabeth threw £1,000 of her own into the pot and lent Frobisher a ship capable of hauling 200 tons of ore from the newly discovered country that she called "Meta Incognita — Land Unknown." Three ships set out in May of 1577 with strict instructions to search for gold, and gold alone.

By late August they had laboriously retrieved their stockpile of black rock. Frobisher took several Inuit hostage, but hopes of trading them for his missing sailors faded after a skirmish that left an Inuit arrow puncture in the admiral's backside.

Returning to England, the cargo was hoarded under quadruple lock in the Tower of London and at Bristol Castle. Controversy over its value raged, but before it was even assayed, a third expedition was mounted. Fifteen ships departed with instructions to establish a settlement and to return with 2,000 tons of ore.

Ice, fog and mistaken navigation delayed their arrival at Kodlunarn ("Island of the White Men") off the coast of Baffin Island. Fortune frowned again when the bark carrying building materials and supplies for the colony sank. Nevertheless, miners hauled aboard tons of ore in wicker osier baskets. Frobisher left a lime and stone cottage on the island, and buried remaining supplies in one of the mine trenches, with hopes of returning to retrieve more gold.

No triumphant welcome awaited Frobisher in England this time. Assayers had pronounced the whole lot of black rock to be fool's gold. Michael Lok was sent to debtor's prison, the company went bankrupt and the Queen found herself out of pocket for her contributions.

Frobisher would never moil in the Arctic again. He went on to serve as a commander in the defeat of the Spanish Armada, a role that earned him a knighthood from his all-forgiving Queen.

The first gold rush in the New World ended when the worthless ore from the Arctic barrens was unceremoniously dumped into Bristol Harbour.

A HATFUL OF GRAIN

DAVID FIFE REAPS WHAT HE SOWS

Otonabee, Upper Canada, 1842 — Scottish settler David Fife had a problem growing a good crop of wheat. There were some years when he lost his whole crop to an early frost, and others when a fungus known as "rust" decimated his production. Fife was experiencing the same problems that had plagued pioneers since European settlers first set seed to sod at Port-Royal in Acadia in 1605, but he was not about to give up.

Farmers had experimented with different varieties of wheat trying to find one suitable to the Canadian climate and growing conditions. They tried varieties that grew everywhere from India to Siberia, but new seed stock was difficult to obtain. Fife believed that northern European varieties might hold the clue. He had a friend who was working as a clerk in Glasgow and he enlisted his aid to obtain seeds direct from the ships that passed through the dockyards.

Security was tight at the Glasgow docks, but somehow the Scottish clerk managed to talk his way into a stroll aboard a ship carrying a bounty of wheat from Danzig (now Gdansk, Poland). While peering into the cargo hold, his hat apparently fell into the bin. No one could criticize the good Scot for wanting to retrieve a perfectly good hat. And no one could have predicted that the handful of wheat kernels that became "accidentally" lodged in the lining of the headgear would change the complexion of Canadian wheat fields from rust to gold before the turn of the century.

In the spring of 1842, David Fife sowed the seeds he had received from Scotland in an experimental garden plot on his farm near what is now Peterborough, Ontario. Except for one, all of the resulting plants perished. The sole survivor produced five fine seed heads. However, reports in the *Canadian Agriculturist* dryly note that two of these "were destroyed by cattle." More lively accounts describe Mrs. Fife confronting a gorging ox in the experimental garden and salvaging just one head — enough seed to fill an egg cup.

The Polish wheat stock thrived in succeeding years and soon neighbours were pleading for seed. It became known as Red Fife, as much for David's red hair as for the seed's own rosy complexion. Less than a decade after its first planting, the plump-berried, rust-resistant strain of wheat was being endorsed by farmers throughout Upper Canada, and it soon spread to spring wheat belts in Michigan, Illinois and Wisconsin. By 1862, the *Canadian Agriculturist* was hailing the golden grain that yielded twenty to thirty bushels per acre as "the glorious Fife ... rather hard to grind, but it makes good flour. Why sir, ten years ago, it would have been considered incredible."

In 1876, Red Fife was planted for the first time in Manitoba's Red River Valley. That year's harvest was to mark the first shipment of wheat out of Western Canada, coinciding with a crop failure in Ontario caused by a dry growing season and a wet harvest. On October 13, the *Winnipeg Free Press* advised that "Steele Brothers, Seedsmen, Toronto, arrived last night ... for the purpose of obtaining 5,000 bushels of Manitoba wheat for seed in Ontario."

The firm of Higgins and Young, "Dealers in Boots and Shoes, Crockery and Glassware," were assigned the task of filling the order that promised to pay farmers eighty cents per bushel. In previous decades, wheat had been traded much as beaver pelts — for goods rather than cash, and the prospect of hard currency caused considerable excitement. When the available grain was finally assembled for shipment at McMillan's Mill on the banks of the Red River, there were only 417 two-bushel, white cotton bags on the dock, less than a fifth of the order. Just one step ahead of freeze-up, the precious cargo moved circuitously by riverboat, rail and lakeboat before reaching Toronto.

By the following year, Red Fife had established a firm following among the Red River settlers and twenty thousand bushels were shipped to eastern buyers on October 17, 1877. One of the contractors was Barclay and Brand of Glasgow, Scotland, which received the first overseas shipment of wheat from the Canadian West. The birth of a viable wheat industry in Canada can be celebrated from that point. Coincidentally, that year also marks the death of David Fife, the red-headed Scot who started an industry with a hatful of grain.

THE GREAT CANADIAN KISSER

MAY IRWIN DELIVERS A FIFTY-FOOT PUCKER

Whitby, Ontario, 1896 — May Irwin was thirty-three years old when she puckered up for the most famous kiss she would ever deliver. The first locking of human lips in cinematic history was a close-up exchange between this Canadian actress/comedienne and American actor James C. Rice. It took inventor Thomas Edison five days to film the fulsome buss, which was promoted as "the first shocker." When *The Fifty-Foot Kiss* made its big screen debut in 1896, sermons and editorials predicted it would lead to moral decline. But few of her childhood friends recognized the famous lips of May Irwin as those of little May Campbell, who had left her hometown of Whitby, Ontario twenty years earlier to sing, dance and amuse on the great stages of the world.

May Campbell became May Irwin around the same time as she reached puberty, simply because the shorter name fit neatly on a marquee. Her father had made a good living in the Ontario logging industry, but he was something of a spendthrift. When he died, May's mother decided to put her young daughters on the stage and presented them at an audition in Buffalo, New York. "It is hard enough being penniless in places like New York or Camden, New Jersey," the buxom entertainer recalled years later, "but nothing to jingle in Whitby, Ontario, is something terrible. Being penniless, my sister, Flo, and I were what you might call in reduced circumstances."

The "Irwin Sisters" were not reduced for long. In 1877, they began a six-year engagement at the top variety house in New York City, Tony Pastor's. By the time she was seventeen, May was married and appearing on "legit" stages in London and Paris. She was hailed as "undeniably the greatest farce actress in America" during the Gay Nineties and became known as "the personification of humour and careless mirth."

Throughout years of heady success, Irwin summered in the Thousand Islands on the St. Lawrence River where she entertained extensively. Each of her guest rooms had twin beds and twin baths. "If there were more plumbing there'd be fewer divorces," she decreed. Irving Berlin is said to have written "Alexander's Ragtime Band" at one of the six grand pianos that decorated the cottage on Irwin Island. May became the first woman to introduce ragtime songs to Broadway. She was also the first white woman to dance the cakewalk on the New York stage — a feat of footwork she learned from the black staff who worked at the tourist hotels in the Islands.

At twenty-five, May was earning $2,500 a week. Unlike her father, she sought out sound investments and purchased substantial real estate in Manhattan. She formed her own company, built her own theatre, and took time out to write a cookbook. Audiences begged for her theme song, "After the Ball is Over," and fretted when she threatened to retire in 1902. "Miss Irwin is a famous fun maker of jolly rotund figure and with a face that reflects the gaiety of nations," wrote one critic. President Woodrow Wilson was so taken with her that he named her his "Secretary of Laughter." In 1925, at the age of sixty-two, she was still a headliner and even Houdini could not upstage her.

When the stock market crashed on October 29, 1929, it took many entertainers and industrialists with it — but May Irwin was not among them. In the spring of that fateful year, she sold all of her real estate, including one lot that reportedly earned her $670,000. While the fortunes of those around her went into a tailspin, she was holding millions in cash.

When she died at seventy-four, her legacy included a body of writing on the art of comedy, as well as her bestselling recipes and several RCA Victor recordings. At her request, she was buried in a red satin dress. It was the final outrageous act of the woman who dared to kiss for the movies.

ONE WITH THE SOIL

CHARLES NOBLE'S BLADE TAKES ROOT ON THE PRAIRIES

Nobleford, Alberta, 1913 — Charles Noble was eighty-four years old when he was inducted into the Alberta Agricultural Hall of Fame. He would probably have been a Hall of Famer earlier, but the Hall was not formed until 1951. It was Noble who gave Western farmers a simple cultivation tool that protected the soil from wind erosion. He invented the Noble Blade.

Charles Sherwood Noble was born in State Center, Iowa. He left school at fifteen to help his father support the family of six boys whose mother died when they were youngsters. He was seventeen when he bought a team of horses and went into business for himself, delivering hay, straw and coal. The following year he began working with his brother, Newell, running a corn-sheller and power-saw operation. He also made time to learn about steam engines and carpentry, and he travelled to Minneapolis to take a business course.

By the time Charles was twenty-three, he had built his own homestead in Knox, South Dakota. Hail and lightning destroyed that dream twice, so one of his brothers urged the industrious Charles to consider Washington State. However, the soil there was not to Charles Noble's liking — and it was his understanding of soil and its care that was to shape his future.

He found what he was looking for in Claresholm, Alberta, in 1902. But it was not just the soil that attracted him to land across the border. Margaret Fraser, the woman who became his wife the following year, had expressed a preference to live Canada.

The region was once home to Blackfoot natives and herds of bison. In his pessimistic 1862 report, British surveyor Captain John Palliser had identified the area as part of "the Great American Desert" and suggested that what became known as the "Palliser Triangle" was "soil worthless" and unsuited for settlement. Of course, he was proved wrong.

In 1909, Noble bought four hundred acres and named the property Grand View Farm. Other acreage was soon added, along with Noble children. It was a life of hard work, and Charles Noble thought nothing of beginning his day at 4 a.m.

On February 14, 1913, the Noble Foundation Company was formed. Its purpose was to "make a contribution to the best utilization of the farmlands of southern Alberta and the prosperity of its people." The Foundation allowed the employees to share in the ownership and trusteeship of the Noble properties.

Boom years followed. Crop yields broke records. In various years, Charles Noble earned the title of World Flax King, World Oat King and World Wheat King. New businesses thrived in the bustling settlement known as "Noble," which was officially named "Nobleford" and incorporated in 1918. The Noble Foundation Company built an office, a General Store and a thirty-room hotel. By then its holdings totalled 33,000 acres, much of it purchased with borrowed money. Ten steam tractors ran day and night breaking up as many as 400 acres a day. Horse-drawn teams carried water to the steamers. Coal was hauled from the local Taber mines.

At one time, a crew of 300 men and 600 mules and horses was working sections of the land. Noble did a cost analysis on the virtues of horsepower, steampower and gasoline tractors and found that horse operations were the most economical. His findings were published in the *Grain Growers Guide*. "We believe that no matter how reasonable engines, parts and fuel may be, it would be a great mistake to neglect the breeding and working of the best type of farm horse," he concluded. Horses, after all, require "much less grief and lower bills for depreciation and repair." Tractors were used as backup for many years.

On the home front, the Noble family was ensconced in a truly noble house by 1918. Built at a cost of $30,000, it included its own 110-volt light plant, water and sewage systems and an indoor swimming pool supplied by its own well.

A drought struck Southern Alberta in 1919 and it lasted for three years. In 1920, the price of wheat tumbled from a peak of $2.20 a bushel to a low of 65 cents. In successive years, the rainfall was too light for a heavy-yielding wheat crop. In 1922, the bondholders and the Bank of Montreal foreclosed, taking the Noble Foundation's $2.5 million in assets to cover a $650,000 debt. Charles Noble had pledged everything except his furniture to support the Foundation. At the age of fifty, he started over.

By 1930, Noble had reacquired his home and more than 7,500 acres. Still, between bank interest and soil drifting, the bank statements of the period contained more red ink than black. Noble's interest in solving the problem of conserving prairie soil and moisture became a passion shared by his sons, Shirley and Gerald. Their mission was to figure out a way to work the soil without turning it. The idea was to cut below the surface, killing weeds, sealing in moisture and leaving the surface stubble of the previous year's crop to form a protective mulch.

In 1935, Noble invented a straight blade cultivator that did the job. Improvements were made, and the straight blade was changed to a V-shape with the convex blade tilting horizontally by 30 degrees, facilitating its use on rolling land conditions. In 1942, patents were obtained and a small plant started manufacturing the Noble Blade. With missionary zeal, Charles Noble demonstrated the implement all over North America, often working in conjunction with Canadian Experimental farms and U.S. Soil Conservationists. The business grew and the cultivator that Noble created was soon joined by a variety of other implements.

"The Chief," as he was known to many of his long-time employees, was also hailed as the "Grand Old Man of Agriculture." He was appointed a member of the Order of the British Empire and granted an honorary Doctorate of Laws from the University of Alberta.

Charles Noble's love of the land was as great then as it had been one summer day in 1917, when he drove over an expanse of prairie near the joining of the Oldman and Little Bow Rivers. He was with his young son, Shirley, who saw nothing much in the land except small herds of antelope and a coyote. Charles paused to examine a few badger and gopher holes that showed the subsoil. Then he drove to

Lethbridge to make an offer to buy the land. Later he explained his reasons to the family, saying simply, "The land had strength and the land lay beautifully."

Charles Noble was the sort of farmer who would know such things.

THE PIE MAN

MACK SENNETT — THE KING OF COMEDY

Hollywood, 1914 — "In Canada, where I was fetched, life was cold and serious. Canadians are not congenitally comic," explained Mikall Sinott, who earned the title "King of Comedy" as Mack Sennett — actor, writer, producer and director of more than one thousand silent slapstick films. The self-described "Canadian farm boy" discovered Charlie Chaplin, invented the Keystone Kops and climaxed virtually all of his films with a wild chase sequence that could involve anything from bathing beauties to rusty bicycles, cats, dogs and babies. He is best known for the physical comedy that he brought to the silver screen, especially the delivery of a custard pie in the face of an unsuspecting subject. "There is a great deal of humour in the combination of surprise and violence," Sennett noted. "A lowering of dignity is always funny."

Mikall Sinnott was born in Danville, Quebec in 1880, the son of Irish parents. The family moved to Connecticut when he was seventeen, and Mikall set his sights on becoming an opera singer, but ended up playing bit parts in vaudeville theatre as "Mack Sennett." One of his first roles was as the back end of a burlesque horse. That auspicious beginning led to bit parts as a five-dollar-a-week actor in the "flickers," where he worked with legendary film director D.W. Griffith at Biograph Studios. He became a screenwriter when he discovered that scripts were worth twenty-five dollars. By 1910, he was writing, directing and acting in an average of two, ten-minute comedies every week.

Sennett founded the Keystone Production Company in 1912. Legend has it that he borrowed the name from a sign he saw at a train station, and that he borrowed the money from a couple of bookies. The "studio" was a twenty-eight-acre lot in the wilds of Southern California, which is now the heart of downtown Los Angeles. The climate was perfect for filming almost every day. In its first year, Keystone turned out 140 films and Mack Sennett made his first million dollars.

Improvisation, innovation and sheer determination fuelled the comedic pace. As Sennett was fond of saying, "It's got to move." In those early days of film, the camera was cranked by hand and the film was edited by the foot. Sennett's early films were one- or two-reelers, lasting ten to twenty minutes. In 1914, he created the first full-length feature comedy motion picture, *Tillie's Punctured Romance*, which starred Marie Dressler from Cobourg, Ontario, Charlie Chaplin (as the city slicker) and Mabel Normand, the love of Sennett's life.

It was Normand who threw that first famous pie. Weary of a long day of filming, the flighty starlet caught her co-star, crosseyed comic Ben Turpin, in her crosshairs and let one fly. "His aplomb vanished in a splurch of goo and his magnificent eyes emerged batting in stunned outrage in all directions," Sennett recalled in his 1954 autobiography *King of Comedy*.

The pie toss became Sennett's trademark and a hallmark of slapstick comedy. "Non anticipation on the part of the recipient of the pastry is the chief ingredient of the recipe," he said. And there were other rules to follow. According to Sennett's instructions, "A mother never gets hit with a custard pie. Mothers-in-law, yes. But mothers, never."

The advent of cartoon short features such as Walt Disney's *Mickey Mouse* and talking pictures such as *The Jazz Singer*, produced by Montrealer Sam Warner, led to Sennett's business failure and fade into obscurity. Abandoned by Mabel Normand because he spent so much time making movies, he stuck by her through a difficult period in which she was under investigation for the unsolved murder of her playboy film director boyfriend, William Desmond Taylor. He was grief-stricken when she died in 1930 at thirty-three, amid rumours of drug problems and in the aftermath of a shooting involving her chauffeur and her gun.

In 1935, a bankrupt Sennett returned to Canada for four years, living in penury on the Quebec property his mother bought with money he sent to her during his heyday of twenty-one-room Hollywood mansions and magnificent yachts. Hollywood did not forget him, however. His protégés included director Frank Capra (*It Happened One Night*, *Mr. Smith Goes to Town*), who started his career as a Keystone "gag-man," and the talents he brought to prominence included Gloria Swanson, Bing Crosby, Carole Lombard and W.C. Fields. In 1937, a special Academy Award was presented to "that master of fun, discoverer of stars, sympathetic, kindly, genius — Mack Sennett."

"Maybe people are paying too much attention to grammar today," Sennett told a reporter in 1959. "I don't think there's too many belly laughs in grammar." A year later, at seventy-six, he died following surgery for a kidney ailment. At the time, he was said to be working on a script — a comedy, no doubt.

BORN OF FIRE AND BLOOD

JOHN MCCRAE'S POEM OF SACRIFICE AND CHALLENGE

Ypres, Belgium, 1915 — As one officer would later recall, the wounded arrived "in batches." Sometimes they fell at the feet of the field physician who struggled to maintain some sense of sanity and some preserve of sanitation in the trenches where wounds could quickly turn to putrefaction. This was Ypres, Belgium, where Canadian troops saw battle for the first time in World War One. It was here, amid the brutal horror of bullet and bayonet injuries and the blue-green death masks of chlorine gas victims, that John McCrae wrote three stanzas which have come to symbolize the ultimate sacrifice and challenge of war.

> *In Flanders fields the poppies blow*
> *Between the crosses, row on row,*
> *That mark our place; and in the sky*
> *The larks, still bravely singing, fly*
> *Scarce heard amid the guns below.*

We are the Dead. Short days ago
We lived, felt dawn, saw sunset glow,
Loved and were loved, and now we lie,
In Flanders fields.

Take up our quarrel with the foe:
To you from failing hands we throw
The torch; be yours to hold it high.
If ye break faith with us who die
We shall not sleep, though poppies grow
In Flanders fields.

As a Major, McCrae was an artillery brigade surgeon during the Second Battle of Ypres. He was forty-two when he jotted the poem in pencil on a page torn from a dispatch pad on May 3, 1915. It was a moment of brief respite in the sixteen-day battle which saw more than six-thousand Canadians killed and wounded. McCrae had left his dressing station at the base of a bank on the Ypres Canal and he was travelling in the back of a field ambulance. Just north of the bridge, there was a field dotted with scarlet poppies and wooden crosses. The day before, McCrae had set a cross in that field to mark the grave of a friend, Lieutenant Alex Helmer of Ottawa.

The doctor had seen the face of battle before. Following his graduation from the University of Toronto, McCrae served as a gunner in the South African War. Returning to Canada in 1900, he was appointed as a fellow in pathology at McGill University and pathologist to Montreal General Hospital. As a physician, he wrote a number of medical textbooks, and privately he wrote poetry, which he submitted to various periodicals.

Volume Two of *Literary History of Canada* describes "In Flanders Fields" as "a restrained, formal flawless expression of Canadian feeling." McCrae's commanding officer, Major General E.W. Morrison, called it a poem "born of fire and blood." The English magazine *Punch* received the poem anonymously and published it in December of 1915.

Colonel McCrae died of pneumonia on January 28, 1918, five days after his appointment as consulting physician to the First British Army. His cross is Number 3 in Row 4 of Plot 4 at Wimereux Communal Cemetery, near Boulogne, France. In memory of him, a perpetual light burns in the garden of his birthplace in Guelph, Ontario, where McCrae House is maintained as a national historic site.

One of John McCrae's comrades, Captain William Boyd — himself a former University of Montreal pathology professor — served five months at the front before joining a field ambulance unit at Ypres. He described the battlefield as a "stricken land, where death stalks you by day and takes you by the arm as you walk the road at night."

It is a wonder that a lark could sing above such grief.

She Did It Her Way

La Bolduc — First Lady of *Chanson*

Montreal, 1929 — Mary-Rose-Anne Travers was a child of thirteen when she left her home in the Gaspésien town of Newport to earn her living in Montreal. Fluently bilingual, she grew up in a large family of English descent, enduring poverty as a way of life, and intuitively understanding music as its escape valve. She learned to play the violin, the harmonica and the accordian, and she was as comfortable with Irish reels as she was with the songs of Acadia.

Mary's decision to leave her home was intended to relieve some financial burden from her family. To finance her trip she fiddled on the main street and sold a popular patent medicine of the day called Red Pills. Arriving in Montreal in 1907, the teenager found work as a household maid. Later she entered a textile mill, working thirteen-hour days for pitiful wages. Shortly after the outbreak of the First World War, she married a plumber, Édouard Bolduc. Illness and poverty plagued their early years. Mary gave birth to thirteen children; however, only four survived.

Madame Bolduc began her performing career out of economic necessity. In her first public appearance, she was a replacement fiddle player in Conrad Gauthier's popular folklore show *Veillées du bon vieux temps*. When Gauthier encouraged her to sing publicly in 1927, she was such a success that he suggested she compose songs of her own.

Day-to-day life became the theme of the songstress known as "La Bolduc." Keenly observant, she found humour in subjects such as insurance agents, mothers-in-law and the police. In "La Grocerie du coin," for example, she gleefully told the public what they already knew was going on at their cornerstore. Her musical advice was to "Watch close when they weigh your meat/ Sometimes they will try to cheat." La Bolduc warned patrons not to fall prey to the distraction of a shopkeeper's yarn and her audiences — recognizing the familiar ruse — howled in delight.

Live performances on radio brought La Bolduc to popular attention. By 1929, she was ready to record. Finding no backers, she paid for studio time herself. Her first record, "La Cusinière" (The Cook), sold an unprecedented 12,000 copies in Quebec. Backers were found and soon La Bolduc was turning out a record almost every month.

The energy and the spirit of hope that La Bolduc brought to her music was a welcome respite in the bleak landscape of the Depression. Her joyous style, embellished by *turlutages* or comic ritonelles produced by clicking her tongue against her palate, made her the idol of the working class. Renowned anthropologist and ethnomusicologist Marius Barbeau found in her songs a "reckless verve and unique twist of tongue in the manner of the singers of the true soil."

She toured tirelessly in Quebec and New England and

produced a total of seventy-four songs on record. In 1937, tragedy struck when a serious car accident ended her tour in Rimouski. In the course of treating her injuries, doctors discovered a cancerous tumour. Four years later, French Canada's first lady of *chanson* died at forty-six.

The musical legacy of La Bolduc has been commemorated by musicans such as Jean "Ti-Jean" Carignan and André Gagnon. In 1994, she was featured on a postage stamp, and her hometown in Newport maintains a permanent exhibit in her honour. New audiences are constantly rediscovering her music.

As CBC Radio's music archivist Adrian Shuman noted in his "discovery" of the chansonnière in 1994, "Her voice turns darkness into sunlight. It has a wonderful earthiness. You smile, and suddenly you feel like doing a jig."

THE WONDER MUSH REVOLUTION

PABLUM — THE GLOP THAT MAKES YOU GROW

Toronto, 1930 — Although its taste has been compared to that of boiled Kleenex and wallpaper paste, the gloppy mush known as Pablum revolutionized pediatric nutrition around the world. It became the first solid food of an entire generation of Canadians. Tons of it have been dutifully ingested, scraped off high chairs and wiped away from sticky cheeks, foreheads and noses. Aside from growing bigger and healthier children, the royalties from this all-Canadian wonder food have helped fund research into everything from a cure for congenital hip disorders to the discovery of the cystic fibrosis gene. Canadian doctors, not marketers, invented Pablum.

Dr. Alan Brown, who served as physician-in-chief of Toronto's Hospital for Sick Children from 1919 to 1951, was determined to bring proper nutrition to the nurseries of the nation. Early in his tenure, he boldly claimed that he could slash the number of infant deaths by half. He accomplished that end with the assistance of research doctors Theodore Drake and Fred Tisdall.

Sixty-five years ago the cereals that babies were fed after mother's milk and sweetened formula were mostly starch. Most of the vitamins, minerals, phosphates and protein contained in the bran and wheat germ had been processed out and fed to livestock. Recognizing this, Fred Tisdall consulted with the poultry department at the Ontario Agriculture College in Guelph, which was developing a healthy feed for chicks. As it turned out, the same natural ingredients were involved for babies; the only difference was quantity.

Back at their lab, Tisdall and Drake invented a vitamin-rich baby biscuit that was "irradiated" under a mercury quartz lamp to add the so-called "sunshine vitamin" D. They introduced their product in a 1930 *Canadian Medical Association Journal*, and it went on to be sold as McCormick's Sunwheat Biscuits, with royalties accruing to fund their ongoing research.

The "big one" was a cereal product Drake stirred up in 1929. Wheat meal, cornmeal and oatmeal masked the flavour of the other ingredients, including bone meal, brewer's yeast and alfalfa. "We had to say we liked it whether we did or not," one hospital colleague advised years later. But adult taste buds were not the target and babies glommed the stuff down.

Drake and Tisdall were en route to Chicago to sell the idea to Quaker Oats when they met up with some friends from Mead Johnson and offered it to them. Mead's Cereal — the precursor to Pablum — was introduced in 1930. It required messy hours of cooking. Ultimately, high-pressure processing refinements were made to create a pre-cooked, vitamin-fortified cereal that was palatable within minutes by adding water or milk.

The concoction was named after the Latin noun *pabulum*, meaning food. In the midst of the Depression, it became an overnight success. There was no waste in preparation, and it cost less than two cents per serving. Convenience aside, Pablum also became a "celebrity baby food," when it was announced that the Dionne quintuplets were being raised on the new wonder cereal. Dr. Alan Brown was one of their consulting physicians.

By the time the patent on Pablum ran out twenty-five years later, Brown's brash pediatric prediction had come true. Nutrition became a recognized component of preventative medicine, and the gooey wonder mush developed by Tisdall and Drake shovelled millions in royalties into the Hospital for Sick Children's Pediatric Research Foundation.

PART SIX

TRANSPORTATION AND COMMUNICATION

HUMPS ALONG THE FRASER

THAT LONG DISTANCE FEELING

PRESS PASS 110

RADIO MAN

THE MAVERICK MUSE OF THE WEST

"JUST ONCE MORE"

THE PICASSO OF BUSH PILOTS

HUMPS ALONG THE FRASER

CAMELS STINK IN THE CARIBOO GOLD RUSH

Cariboo Trail, British Columbia, 1862 — The headline in the Victoria *Colonist-Times* read simply "The Camels are Coming." Sure enough, they were. Twenty-three of them, to be precise, landed on the docks at Esquimalt in April of 1862. They were not particularly attractive or hospitable camels after their long journey. They had travelled from Manchurian China, across the Pacific to San Francisco, where a Seton Portage rancher named John Calbraith purchased them for $6,000 on behalf of another Victoria native, Frank Laumeister and his two partners. The hope was that the two-humped Bactrian behemoths would be worth their weight in gold on the Cariboo trail.

The Cariboo was crawling with gold-crazed miners, dreamers and adventurers who went to incredible lengths to travel the tortuous Fraser Canyon Route to Quesnel Forks in the British Columbia interior. Governor James Douglas had started a wagon road north of Yale, and road gangs of Chinese workers using pickaxes and shovels had toiled to create a passable route. This was territory explorer Simon Fraser called "so wild" that he could not find words for it. However, when Governor Douglas inspected progress on his "road," he optimistically noted that "Passes of ominous fame, so notorious in the history of the country have lost their terrors." However, according to one traveller, what passed for a trail was nothing more than "mud, stones [and] trees falling in every direction."

This was where the surefooted, two-toed camels were supposed to save the day. Freight costs to the Cariboo from Victoria and New Westminster were skyrocketing. Hundreds of mules worked the trails, carrying packs loaded with everything from candles to pianos. It could take a plodding mule train weeks to make its destination, and many a mule never made it — tumbling down the canyon walls onto the rocks below.

Camel-caravan impresario Laumeister had been advised that his camels could carry half-ton loads and travel almost twice as fast as mules. In earlier decades, one-humped dromedaries had been imported for army use in Texas and they had been used in the exploration of California deserts. Mules were expensive to feed, but a thrifty camel was supposed to be able to forage for subsistence and go for six to ten days without water. In theory, the "ship of the desert" was ideally suited to become the freight train of the gold rush.

Two of the camels that landed in Victoria stayed there. A calf and its mother (dubbed "Her Camelship") were turned loose in Beacon Hill Park where they came as quite a surprise to the unsuspecting. The pack camels were shipped by steamer to New Westminster and the start of the trail.

At the outset, the camels appeared to perform well,

although their load capacity was less than anticipated. After a few weeks on the job, the *Times-Colonist* reported, "They are acclimated, and will eat anything from a pair of pants to a bar of soap." The true test came when the camels hit the mountains, where rocky pathways tore into their tender toe pads. Improvised boots made from canvas and rawhide were not much help.

The real downfall of the camels was their smell, which was as intolerable to humans as it was to mules and horses. Mules would bray incessantly and stop dead in their tracks if they so much as sensed — or scented — a camel in the vicinity. Horses would panic. Camels were also prone to panic. On June 30, some fur traders startled a young camel on the trail and it slid over the edge to its demise, accompanied by a full load of Scotch whisky.

Soon there was havoc. Muleteers and horse-owners threatened to take their case to Chief Justice Matthew Baillie Begbie, and there were rumours of a petition to ask Governor Douglas to order the removal of all camels from the Cariboo. None of this was necessary. The camel syndicate withdrew the unhappy, ungainly creatures due to performance failure.

The camels were dispersed in various ways. Eight of them were let loose at Lac La Hache, about halfway between Lillooet and Quesnel, where they died during the winter. A few went to America, selling for a mere thirty-five dollars each. Some were eaten by hungry settlers, one of whom is said to have commented that "camel flesh is delicious when fried." That may have been an acquired taste or one determined by necessity, since there were few takers when camel was placed on the menu of a Cariboo Trail restaurant.

One member of the failed camel syndicate, Henry Ingram, took his losses with him and ended up with three camels grazing on his ranch at Grande Prairie (now West-wold). In 1864 he sold 181.8 kilograms (404 pounds)of camel meat to the Hudson's Bay Company in Kamloops in exchange for tools. That accounted for two of his camels.

The third camel stayed on the Ingram farm as a house-hold pet and it outlived Henry Ingram, who died in 1879. Every spring, the camel was sheared and its hair was used to stuff pillows and mattresses. Local children enjoyed tak-ing rides on the gentle creature. Finally, in extreme old age, the last of the Cariboo camels died in 1905. Apparently it simply leaned against a tree and died on its feet.

There are stories that claim a few wild camels survived until 1910, and an alleged bush-sighting near Kamloops in 1925 fuelled speculation that camels might be making a comeback. One thing is certain: camels were not invited to participate in the Klondike gold rush.

That Long Distance Feeling

Phoning and Flying with Mr. and Mrs. Bell

Brantford, Ontario, 1876 — When Alexander Graham Bell achieved international fame as the inventor of the telephone, Scotland claimed him for his birthright, America claimed him for the citizenship he took in 1882, and Canada also demanded a piece of the action.

"Of this you may be sure, the telephone was invented in Canada," Bell wrote and said many times. "It was made in the United States." According to Bell, Brantford, Ontario was justifiably dubbed "the telephone city," because it was there, at nearby Tutelo Heights, that he conceived his invention in 1874. The Bell family had come to Canada four years earlier, hoping to find relief for Alexander, their sickly twenty-three-year-old son who was fighting with tuberculosis. Two of his brothers had already succumbed to the disease. "I went to Canada to die," Bell recalled later, but the change in geography proved therapeutic.

Much of Bell's research took place in the United States. It is a good bet that every school child in North America learns that the first telephone conversation began with Bell's request, "Mr. Watson, come here I need you." It happened in Boston. Five months later, on August 3, 1876, the language of communication elevated substantially when Hamlet's "To be or not to be" soliloquy was recited between two buildings in Brantford. The following week, the long distance feeling became a reality when Bell's father spoke to his son over telegraph wires from Brantford to Robert White's Book and Shoe Store more than twelve kilometres (7.4 miles) away in Paris, Ontario. That first long distance phone call lasted for three hours, consisting largely of songs that ranged from the sacred to the profane.

Bell returned to Canada every chance he got. Once he came to borrow money and the result was one of the most classic business blunders in history. Senator George Brown, a Father of Confederation and the editor of the *Globe* newspaper, was a friend of the Bells and he kept a farm near Tutelo Heights. In the summer of 1875, Bell returned to the family home to rest and recuperate from his extensive American experiments — and to raise some cash. He had fallen in love with Mabel Hubbard, a former student of his at a Boston school for the deaf and the daughter of one of his principal American backers. But his inventions had side-tracked him from making a daily living. In Canada, he asked Brown for approximately three hundred dollars to tide him over until the telephone made him his fortune.

Brown and his brother, Gordon, agreed to provide Bell with fifty dollars per month, in exchange for half the British Empire and foreign patents. Brown was to file these patents when he went to England in January, 1876. But in England the specifications stayed in his trunk, suggesting that Brown was concerned about being associated with a crackpot idea.

Bell's future father-in-law finally gave up on the Canadian and filed Bell's patent application in Washington on Valentine's Day, 1876, just hours before a rival presented a similar idea. George Brown blew one of the biggest paydays in history.

Bell married Mabel five months later. When he took his bride to Brantford, Mrs. Bell Sr. broke an oatcake over her daughter-in-law's head following a Scottish tradition to ensure that the bride would never go hungry in her husband's home. There seemed little chance of that. Three years later, Bell was awarded the $50,000 Volta Prize. Despite more than six hundred legal challenges to his patents, he won every one and became a wealthy man, a prodigious inventor and a laudable philanthropist.

In 1885, Bell began acquiring land nead Baddeck, Nova Scotia on Cape Breton Island where he established a summer home, Beinn Bhreagh (Gaelic for "beautiful mountain"). The telephone had been just the beginning of Bell's invention spree. He was also the father of the phonograph record, but he was most proud of his work on behalf of the oral education of the deaf. He served as president of the National Geographic Society and his never-ending curiosity saw him investigate everything from radar to breeding sheep that would consistently produce twin lambs.

At Beinn Bhreagh, Bell pursued his interest in flight, experimenting with monumental kites. In 1907, Mabel Bell became the first woman to establish and endow a research organization, the Aerial Experimental Association, whose objective was "to get into the air." This culminated in the first airplane flight in the British Commonwealth by the Silver Dart in 1909.

Bell may have taken American citizenship, but when he

died in 1922 he was a citizen of the world. He was buried at Baddeck, in a pine coffin built by the men who worked in his laboratory. The consummate inventor wore the medal of the French Legion of Honour to his grave, which was carved into Cape Breton rock and flanked by the British and American flags. While a Highland piper skirled him to his rest, every telephone in North America was silenced for two minutes.

PRESS PASS 110

KIT COLEMAN — WAR CORRESPONDENT

Cuba, 1898 — "After nearly three months of despairing to get here, the great force we call will has conquered. I am looking at the hills of Cuba," read the dispatch to the Toronto *Mail and Empire* from press correspondent pass 110, who had arrived at the scene of the Spanish-American War. More than 130 members of the press had applied to "cover" the war, but Number 110 was a distinctly different voice. It belonged to the first woman in the world to become an accredited war correspondent. She was a thirty-four-year-old reporter from Canada, who became internationally renowned as "Kit" Coleman.

The bronze-haired daughter of Irish gentry, Kathleen Blake was born at Castle Blakeny near Galway, Ireland, in 1864. Educated at Dublin and in Belgium, she was unhappily married at sixteen. Widowhood at nineteen propelled her to a new beginning in Canada, where she remarried and

settled in Winnipeg. Now a mother of two, she was wid-
owed again in 1888 and moved to Toronto. The following
year she submitted a story about an organ grinder to *Saturday Night* magazine, which led to a job at the *Mail* where
she established a page for female readers called the
"Woman's Kingdom."

Over the next twenty-two years, "Kit of the Mail"
attracted readers of both sexes. One of her biggest fans was
Prime Minister Wilfrid Laurier. Topics ranged from divorce
to Western imperialism and from recipes to racism. She
dished out advice to the lovelorn and wrote columns with
titles such as "Waists of English Actresses," and "Is Marriage
a Failure?" Her popularity was such that the *Mail and Empire*
sent her to cover the Diamond Jubilee of Queen Victoria
and the Chicago World's Fair. To other women of the press,
she was a role model. In 1904, she founded the Canadian
Women's Press Club while on a junket with a dozen colleagues to the St. Louis Exposition. Surprisingly, she was
opposed to women's suffrage, calling its exponents "platform women."

When America declared war against Spain over the status of Cuba on April 25, 1898, Coleman caught war fever.
Initially, she tried to persuade the Red Cross to let her tag
along — undercover — as a member of the nursing staff.
When that failed, she cajoled U.S. Secretary of War Russell
Alger into accrediting her, with the provision that she stay
with missionary or relief columns and avoid army camps.

When she arrived in Tampa, Florida, looking for a boat
that would take her to Cuba, a legion of male reporters
thought it a sensation. London *Daily Mail* correspondent
Charles Hands described her as a "tall, healthy youngish
lady with a quiet self-reliant manner and an enterprising
look." Coleman told him that she knew he thought she was

"ridiculous," but she did not much care. "I'm going through to Cuba," she told him, "and not all the old Generals in the old army are going to stop me." While she looked for passage, she wrote about what she saw of the 17,000 ill-prepared troops readying for battle. She called these lightweight stories the "guff." They included everything from interviews with Canadians who formed part of Theodore Roosevelt's soon-to-be-legendary Rough Riders to comments on the Canadian nickel used on American gunboats.

Unlike her male counterparts, Kit was trying to cover a war on a shoestring budget. Top American correspondents carried gold to cover expenses, but the impoverished Coleman was reduced to mailing most of her columns back to her editors. She sent only three telegraphs, and one of those landed her in hot water.

When troops assembled on the Tampa docks for the invasion, she wired the news in a coded message to her *Mail and Empire* editor. Later she wrote, "As I marched triumphantly from the telegraph office thinking how bright and clever I was to get off the news to my paper ... a Secret Service officer touched me on the shoulder, 'I arrest you,' he said." Eventually, she was released and went back to the business of trying to arrange passage to Cuba.

On August 8, 1898, the front page of the *Mail and Empire* proudly declared "Kit Reaches Cuba's Shores." The story was datelined July 28 — the day that Coleman *left* Cuba. All told, she spent approximately one week observing a war that had all but ended by July 17.

Her biggest story of the war was about the trip home. It began aboard a cockroach-infested ship crammed with wounded soldiers in the care of a medical student who had no medicine. Coleman and three other reporters provided the sick with quinine capsules and shared their field supplies.

Off the coast of Florida, the "horror ships" were quarantined for a week and conditions worsened. Despite the gruesomeness of the scene, Coleman accompanied 350 wounded on a ship bound for New York. She helped the sick and got the story.

Five months after her adventures in Cuba, Coleman addressed the International Press Union in Washington and told them, "If ever a time comes when swords are beaten into ploughshares and spears into pruning hooks, it will be for one reason, because the wielders of pens were not less earnest and may we say, not less heroic, than the wielders of deadlier weapons." Believing that the press would play a powerful role in eliminating war through the immediacy of front-line reportage was one thing, participating was another. Coleman announced that if another war came along "this pioneer woman war correspondent will stay home."

Although she offered penetrating assessments of the brutal inanity of conflicts in South Africa, Russia and China, she did not venture back to the front. Instead, she married a mining company doctor and moved to Copper Cliff in northern Ontario, where she lived and wrote for three years. When they moved to Hamilton, she resumed feature writing — focusing on crime stories. Her biggest "scoop" came in 1904, when she scored an exclusive interview with Canadian con-artist Cassie Chadwick, who styled herself as the illegitimate daughter of American industrialist Andrew Carnegie.

In 1911, the *Mail and Empire* asked Coleman to add a daily column to her workload, with no increase in pay. It was too much to ask, even of a woman who once suggested to one of her advice-seeking readers, "It is an honour to write for nothing, if you write well." For years she had been earning thirty-five dollars a week, a paltry sum by American standards. She quit her job and began syndicating "Kit's

Column" for five dollars a piece to various newspapers, but never again to the *Mail and Empire*.

Mabel Burkholder, a member of the Hamilton Women's Press Club who met Kit in 1891, has suggested that in America, "She would have been considered the most brilliant newspaper woman on the continent." Burkholder concluded that, "Kit was handicapped by being too big for her position, and too progressive for her times."

Kit Coleman died of pneumonia on May 16, 1915. It was her fifty-first birthday.

RADIO MAN

REGINALD FESSENDEN — THE FATHER OF RADIO

Brant Rock, Massachusetts, 1900 — Before any event involving the transmission of sound begins, chances are that someone steps up to the microphone to test the system by intoning the words "one, two, three, four...." The banality of this announcement has historic roots — those four little words were the first ever to be broadcast by a human voice. They were transmitted by Canadian inventor Reginald Aubrey Fessenden on December 23, 1900, 354 days before Guglielmo Marconi, the alleged "father of radio," managed to transmit a mere Morse code "S" from a hill in Newfoundland to a receiving station in Britain. Fessenden also initiated the first two-way transatlantic voice transmission in 1906, the same year that he delivered the first ever radio broadcast.

Reginald Fessenden may be one of the least-lauded geniuses Canada has ever produced. Born in a small town near Sherbrooke, Quebec, in 1865, he was teaching Greek and French at Bishop's University at the age of sixteen. In his spare time, he studied mathematics. By 1886, he had sufficient confidence in his comprehension of science to solicit an introduction to American electrical pioneer Thomas Edison. Without practical experience, Edison rejected the brash Canadian, but Fessenden inveigled his way into a job testing the maestro's lighting wires in the streets of Manhattan, and ultimately into a position in Edison's research laboratory.

"An inventor must never be intimidated by what appear to be facts when he knows they are not," Fessenden once noted. It was that guiding principle that allowed him to unravel the electrical relations of the atom decades before his contemporaries. Consequently, he provided Edison with an insulating compound for electrical wire, negating the problem of "hot wires" that plagued the fledgling lighting industry. When Edison went broke, Fessenden went to work for George Westinghouse, for whom he built a longer-lasting, economical light bulb.

With more than five hundred inventions to his credit, Fessenden's output was prodigious. At the turn of the century, he cut a colourful swath in the American scientific community with his flame red beard, sweeping black cloak and irrepressible curiosity. As legend has it, his continuous-wave radio theory first dawned on him in 1896. He was en route by train from Toronto to his uncle's home in Peterborough, where he intended to take a vacation from the wireless transmission theorizing he had been doing as the Chair of electrical engineering at the University of Pittsburgh.

After a stint with the U.S. Weather Service, Fessenden found backing for a full-fledged research station at Brant Rock near Boston. Although he was supposed to be concentrating on telegraphy, he secretly devoted himself to radio.

The first transatlantic voice message was accidentally received by his assistant in Scotland, who heard voices while he was listening for dots and dashes. Fessenden followed this unacknowledged achievement with his historic radio broadcast.

Preparations involved adjustments at the peak of a 400-foot transmitting tower, which Fessenden undertook to do himself. He had not, however, calculated accommodating his considerable girth in the tower cylinder. Fortunately, he had already invented a primitive version of the pocket pager, which was built into the headgear of his employees. When their buzzers went off, they discovered the portly Fessenden lodged in the passage. The only way to extricate the wedged wunderkind was to strip off his clothing and rub his body with grease.

On Christmas Eve, 1906, sailors on United Fruit Company cargo ships were monitoring for Morse code messages as they steamed northward from the Caribbean. Instead, they were treated to a one-man variety show. Fessenden played "O Holy Night" on the violin, sang and read a biblical passage before signing off with "Merry Christmas." Letters from incredulous shipboard radio operators confirmed the success of the experiment.

Reginald Fessenden was not the astute businessman or self-promoter that Marconi proved to be. Although the Canadian government endowed Marconi with $80,000 and granted him exclusive rights to build radio stations in Canada, Fessenden could not even get a teaching job at McGill University. Nevertheless, when war broke out he volunteered his services to the Canadian government and contributed everything from an improved internal combustion engine to tracer bullets for machine guns to the sonic depth finder.

A paucity of funds plagued the inventor, and violations of his patents resulted in countless legal battles. By Fessenden's accounting, reparations amounted to $60 million. So it was a minor victory when the U.S. Radio Trust conceded in 1928 with a payment of $2.8 million. Fessenden retired to Bermuda, where he died four years later.

"It sometimes happens that one man can be right against the world," remarked the *New York Herald Tribune*. "Professor Fessenden was that man."

THE MAVERICK MUSE OF THE WEST

UNCORKING THE CONSCIENCE OF
BOB "EYE-OPENER" EDWARDS

Calgary, 1915 — There are those who believe that if newspaper editor Bob Edwards had concentrated more on his own aggrandizement and less on the local tavern, he could have become as famous as Mark Twain. As it happened, the boisterous newspaperman's remarkable wit and political tenacity stood him in good stead as a pathfinder for truth. That he was one of a kind in his profession is undisputed. When this editor who rarely edited himself died in 1922, he was voted the most colourful pioneer in Western Canada by his peers. "People are always ready to admit a man's ability after he gets there," remains one of Edwards's oft-quoted pronouncements.

Born in Scotland to a publishing family of some repute, Edwards emigrated to Wyoming in 1894 after graduating from Glasgow University. Three years later, the impetuous thirty-three-year-old had settled in Wetaskiwin, Alberta, where he launched his first newspaper — a "corker" that he planned to call *The Wetaskiwin Bottle Works* until saner minds prevailed. An itinerant publisher, he settled into a groove when he founded his most famous newspaper, the *Eye-Opener*, in High River, Alberta. His satirical and sarcastic pokes were endured for several years until "the church incident" of 1904, wherein he substituted a recorded hymn with the popular ditty "Just Because She Made Them Goo-Goo Eyes." Shortly afterward, the paper was relocated in Calgary.

Direct news reporting was not of particular interest to Edwards. He preferred to expose hypocrisy and snobbery — his lampooning "Social Notes" bordered on the hysterical. "The family of Mr. and Mrs. W.S. Stott, Eleventh Ave. West, all had the mumps last week," he once reported. "A swell time was had by all. Mr. Stott will not be able to deliver his address today at the Rotary convention much to the relief of those who have heard him speak." He mocked the two-boat Canadian Navy, denounced Alberta Premier A.L. Sifton as a "liar," and once proclaimed that a statesman was "a dead politician, and what this country needs is more of them."

Always skipping the razor edge of libel, Edwards's *Eye-Opener* soon had a circulation that was greater than the population of Calgary. It boasted readers across North America who followed the adventures of delicious fictitious characters such as Albert Buzzard-Cholomondeley, remittance man. Still, Edwards remained constantly in debt and constantly facing the bottom of a bottle at the hotel bar that he frequented with illustrious pals lawyer Paddy Nolan, meat baron Pat Burns and ranch king George Lane.

The crunch of conscience pursued Edwards, however. When Alberta faced a prohibition plebiscite in 1915, the "wets" are said to have solicited his editorial support by offering him almost ten thousand dollars. The "drys" requested the same consideration, but had nothing financial to offer. Despite his personal proclivity, Edwards surprised those who thought his backing was "in the bottle" by devoting an entire issue of the *Eye-Opener* to antibooze editorials and columns. He wrote, "In a word, there is Death in the Cup and if this Act is likely to have the effect of dashing the Cup from the drunkard's hand, for God's sake, let us vote for it." When the issue was published, Edwards was confined to a hospital bed sleeping off a bout with the demon he had condemned. The temperance vote won, and Alberta remained dry until 1923.

As a maverick publisher, Edwards crusaded for soil conservation, old age pensions, votes for women, senate reform and a host of visionary social issues. Despite his derision of politicians, he was elected to the provincial legislature in 1921, but he attended only one sitting before his death.

"I live with a sort of secret hope that between drunks I'm doing something to give this new West an individuality," Edwards is reported to have confided. He had a police escort to his grave and his young wife laid him to rest with the last issue of the *Eye-Opener* and a flask filled with whisky.

"JUST ONCE MORE"

THE UNFORGETTABLE *BLUENOSE*

Lunenburg, Nova Scotia, 1921 — A wooden sailing boat, an iron captain and the salt-spray of the ocean — put them all together and you have a snapshot of Canada's great age of sail. It is an image that has jangled in the pockets of Canadians since 1937, when the schooner *Bluenose* took its place on the ten-cent coin. Unforgettable and unbeatable, the ship and her captain, Angus Walters, were a winning team — the crowning achievement of an Atlantic tradition.

She was a saltbank schooner and he was a fisherman skipper. As a working fishing vessel, the *Bluenose* still holds the record for the single largest catch of fish ever landed in Lunenburg. But make no mistake, she was also built for speed.

In 1920, Senator William Dennis, publisher of the *Halifax Herald*, instigated a series of races to challenge the best of the American and Canadian fishing fleets. That year the International Fishermen's Trophy was won by a Yankee schooner from Gloucester, Massachusetts. Lunenburgers did not take the loss lightly, and Angus Walters was a quintessential Lunenburger. That winter, he helped sell 350 shares at $100 a piece and work began at the Smith and Rhuland shipyards on a boat described as "deep-bellied" and "spoon-bowed." Its designer, Halifax marine architect William Roue, had a committee of interested parties to contend with in the planning of the 43-metre (143-foot) craft. Walters had a controlling interest, so he made some modifications of his own, including raising the bow by about half an arm's length.

"My crew ain't midgets," he blustered when the hull was raised and he found the headroom so limited that even the diminutive captain would have been forced to stoop.

On March 26, 1921, the *Bluenose* was launched. Her christening title, a traditional nickname for Nova Scotians, was a natural choice. She was crafted by Nova Scotians and she was built almost entirely from wood grown in the province.

After a season on the Grand Banks where she proved herself to be the highliner of the fleet, *Bluenose* was given a new coat of paint and rigged for racing. Tall and lean, her copious sails billowed like wings over the water and her great bow rode high over whitecaps. That fall the International Fishermen's Trophy returned to Nova Scotia, never to fall into American hands again.

Only one boat ever faced its stern to the Bluenose at a formal finish line. The *Gertrude L. Thebaud*, a freshly minted, lithesome schooner owned by a syndicate of wealthy Bostonians challenged the toast of Lunenberg to an unofficial racing series in the autumn of 1930. Although his beloved schooner had been hampered by ill-fitting sails, Captain Walters took full responsibility for the loss saying, "They didn't beat the *Bluenose*. They beat me."

The defeat was avenged the following year, when the

Thebaud crossed the line in the International Fishermen's Series more than a full half hour after the *Bluenose.*

The schooner became a celebrity and an ambassador. In 1933, thousands of visitors saluted her grace at Chicago's Century of Progress Exposition. Two years later, Walters and his crew set out from Lunenburg for Plymouth, England, the same port that Sir Francis Drake once sailed from. The occasion was the Silver Jubilee of King George V and Queen Mary. The King apparently took a fancy to the saltbanker and invited Angus to meet him aboard the royal yacht *Victoria and Albert.*

"He was a very nice, ordinary sort of fella," Walters told reporters, adding that they "chewed the rag for a while." Afterward, the King sent word that he wished to inspect the *Bluenose,* but other duties prevailed. Walters was sorry about that; he had gone to the trouble of obtaining a bottle of whisky so that he could entertain the King in style.

The *Bluenose* was seventeen when she confronted the *Gertrude L. Thebaud* in what was to be her final racing series — a challenge spread over five races off the Boston coast. The pair were locked in a tie on October 26, 1938. Millions listened to their radios and a huge crowd watched from shore as the two schooners matched each other across the water, with the *Bluenose* running a scant lead thanks to the experienced manoeuvring of her captain. Victory was just minutes away when a halyard block gave way. Repairs were out of the question.

With the *Thebaud* charging forward to take advantage of her opponent's injury, Walters did what he had always done to the *Bluenose.* He talked to her and she responded. "Just once more!" he was heard crying to the great but aged saltbanker. That exhortation, and a fortuitous gust of wind, was all it took.

The coveted International Fishermen's Cup was awarded to the *Bluenose* permanently. At the celebrations in Lunenburg, Captain Walters said simply, "The wood that can beat the *Bluenose* ain't been planted yet."

Captain Walters retired from the sea to tend his dairy business, but all the while he harboured the dream of preserving the *Bluenose* as a tribute to the age of sail that had passed with the advent of diesel engines and with war looming. In 1940, the fading schooner faced the disgrace of public auction over unpaid bills. Walters mortgaged his home to buy out the shareholders and wrest the Queen of the Atlantic fleet from the sherrif's hands. When he was finally forced to sell her to a freighting firm, Walters said he felt as though he had lost a family member.

The thoroughbred became a pack horse, plodding between the islands of the West Indies carrying bananas and rum. In January of 1946, her back was broken on a coral reef off Haiti, where the *Bluenose* was abandoned. The *Halifax Herald* called the ignominy of her death "a national shame."

In 1963, a replica of the *Bluenose* was launched amid great fanfare. Fittingly, at the Lunenburg christening, Angus Walters was made the Honorary Captain of the *Bluenose II*.

The Picasso Of Bush Pilots

"Punch" Dickins Wings It With Style

Fort Resolution, Northwest Territories, 1929 — The image of the Canadian bush pilot is one that is often grounded in a romantic vision of goggled men in flowing scarves spiriting small aircraft through the wilderness skies of the North. In such an easy fairy tale, Clennell Haggerston "Punch" Dickins could have been the model. Hollywood-handsome with trim jet-black hair and the face of a curious boy, Dickins was the first pilot to survey the unmapped Barren Lands of the Northwest Territories. His legend grew to be so synonymous with northern flight that an Inuit who was giving testimony in an Aklavik court once struggled to find the proper English word for "airplane," before finally hitting on the only description that seemed just right — "Punch Dickins."

Dickins was nine years old when his family moved from Portage la Prairie, Manitoba, to Edmonton, Alberta. He enlisted at the age of seventeen and ended up serving with the Royal Flying Corps during World War I. Dickins honed his skills under perilous conditions. During his seven-month service in France, the flying teenager was credited with the destruction of seven enemy aircraft and earned the Distinguished Flying Cross for gallantry.

In 1921, Dickins joined the Canadian Air Force where he spent six years testing aircraft under winter conditions, flying forestry patrols and conducting photographic surveys. His bush flying career took off in 1927 when he joined Western Canadian Airways and started piloting prospectors over uncharted wilderness.

One such trip took him along the east shore of Great Bear Lake where his passenger, miner Gilbert LaBine, noted a curious glow emanating from the sheer rock cliffs of Echo Bay. The lustre proved to be a mixture of silver, copper and pitchblende, an ore that contains radium and uranium. The discovery became the Eldorado Mine, providing the resources that vaulted Canada into the nuclear age.

Flying north of the sixtieth parallel required extraordinary navigational skills. In August 1928, Dickins flew a prospecting party on a twelve-day trip that stretched over nearly 6,499 kilometres (3,960 miles). All told, they spent thirty-seven hours in the air, much of it over unmapped territory. Piloting over the eerie tundra landscape of the Barrens from Chesterfield Inlet on Hudson Bay to the western reaches of Saskatchewan's Lake Athabasca, Dickins relied largely on sight to navigate, since the proximity of the magnetic pole rendered his compass useless.

"This was over the real Barren Lands," he noted in his journal, "from the time we left Baker Lake we never saw a living thing until getting near the tree line again, when a few birds were seen. The tracks of caribou could be seen also."

Using other means of travel, such a trip would have taken at least a year and a half.

That January, Punch Dickins was asked to explore the possibility of establishing a regular mail service to far northern communities. Since the railway line ended at Fort McMurray, remote settlements along the Mackenzie and Athabasca Rivers received their mail by dog sled once or twice each winter. Airmail deliveries would end the loneliness and isolation, connecting the people of the north to the southern world which they called "Outside."

The first test flight ended in a farmer's field outside of Edmonton when ice particles formed in the plane's carburetor, forcing Dickins to land. Then a blizzard intervened. However, word of the experimental flight created great excitement in the North, and when Dickins finally made his first stop at Fort Chipewyan everyone in town showed up to greet him. They had cleared the snow on a stretch of Lake Athabasca and defined a "landing strip" with fresh-cut spruce trees.

On the return leg of the trip, Dickins and his engineer Lew Parmenter ran into trouble near Fort Resolution on Great Slave Lake. Landing in swirling snow, the undercarriage of the plane hit rough ice. No one was injured, but the fuselage was damaged and the propeller blades were bent out of whack.

Employing the improvisation skills that became a hallmark of bush pilots everywhere, Dickins and Parmenter scrounged a piece of waterpipe from a local priest to repair the fuselage. With moderate pressure, one of the propeller blades was coaxed back into shape, but the other one was badly twisted and snapped off, leaving it more than a hands-length shorter than its companion. Undaunted, the pilots cut the healthy blade to match the size of its diminished companion. Punch taxied the Fokker Super Universal across the ice and found that it could pick up speed. They flew out that afternoon.

Dickins's career was punctuated with adventure and innovation. During World War II he served as the operations manager of Ferry Command and managed six flight schools as part of the British Commonwealth Air Training Plan. After the war, he joined de Havilland Aircraft, where he was instrumental in marketing Canadian-made Beaver aircraft worldwide. An Alberta lake is named after him, and he was the first inductee into Canada's Aviation Hall of Fame in Wetaskiwin. According to fellow flyer Grant McConachie, who worked with Dickins during the early days of Canadian Pacific Airlines, "Of all those pioneer flyers, Dickins stands alone.... One might call him the Picasso of bush pilots."

When Punch died in 1995 at the age of ninety-six, his family requested that his ashes be scattered along the Mackenzie River by his friend, another legendary bush pilot and aviation pioneer, Max Ward.